SO MUCH TO SAY

20 YEARS ON THE ROAD
DAVE MATTHEWS BAND

NIKKI VAN NOY

A TOUCHSTONE BOOK
PUBLISHED BY SIMON & SCHUSTER

NEW YORK LONDON TORONTO SYDNEY

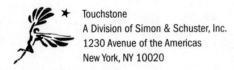

Touchstone
A Division of Simon & Schuster, Inc.
1230 Avenue of the Americas
New York, NY 10020

Copyright © 2011 by Nikki Van Noy

First Touchstone trade paperback edition June 2011

Touchstone and colophon are registered trademarks of Simon & Schuster, Inc.

For information about special discounts for bulk purchases, please contact Simon & Schuster Special Sales at 1-866-506-1949 or business@simonandschuster.com.

The Simon & Schuster Speakers Bureau can bring authors to your live event. For more information or to book an event contact the Simon & Schuster Speakers Bureau at 1-866-248-3049 or visit our website at www.simonspeakers.com.

Designed by Ruth Lee-Mui

Manufactured in the United States of America

10 9 8 7 6 5 4 3 2 1

Library of Congress Cataloging-in-Publication Data

Van Noy, Nikki.
    So much to say : Dave Matthews Band : twenty years on the road / by Nikki Van Noy.
        p. cm.
    Includes discography.
    1. Dave Matthews Band. 2. Rock groups—United States. 3. Rock music fans. I. Title.
II. Title: Dave Matthews Band.
    ML421.D38V36 2011
    781.66092'2—dc22
    [B]
                                                              2011000427

ISBN 978-1-4391-8273-4
ISBN 978-1-4391-8275-8 (ebook)

FOR MY LITTLE BROTHER AND FAVORITE MUSICIAN,

NICK,

WHO TAUGHT ME THAT TWO THINGS ARE ETERNAL:

LOVE AND MUSIC.

CONTENTS

xiii Introduction: Hello, How Are You Doing Today?

1 Chapter 1: An Evening Spent Dancing: It's You and Me

13 Chapter 2: Getting Started: Things Were Quiet Then

35 Chapter 3: The Little Red Van: Drive In, Drive Out, I'm Leaving

59 Chapter 4: The Big Three: I Can See Three Corners from This Corner

97 Chapter 5: The Album That Wasn't: Out of My Hands

125 Chapter 6: Searching for the Sound: Till I Get to the End of This Tunnel

151 Chapter 7: LeRoi Holloway Moore: If I Die Before My Time

165 Chapter 8: LeRoi's Legacy: Drinking Big Whiskey While We Dance and Sing

186 Chapter 9: Hitting the Road: Would You Like to Dance Around the World with Me?

208 Chapter 10: Looking Back: I Find It Hard to Explain How I Got Here

213 Discography (1993–2010)

219 Acknowledgments

SO MUCH TO SAY

When you get old and grey and you think back on your better days, just imagine the good feeling of looking at your Dave Matthews Band T-shirt and just recollecting, reminiscing . . . going back in your mind to those fun days. When your children are freaking out on some mediocre musician who's popular for a short time on the radio, you can say, "I remember when I was in college, before I became the president of IBM, I remember Boyd Tinsley *right there* at Zollman's Pavilion. And every time I look at that T-shirt I just remember when I was young and the world was beautiful."

—LeRoi Moore
Zollman's Pavilion /
Lexington, Virginia,
May 31, 1993

HELLO, HOW ARE YOU DOING TODAY?

Fifteen years ago, on October 2, 1996, I walked into Boston's Fleet Center, completely unaware that my life was about to change. To be honest, I wasn't all that thrilled to be there in the first place. I had a room-mate in college who wouldn't stop talking about Dave Matthews Band (DMB) and their live show, which she swore was just the greatest, most fun thing ever. To say I was wary is an understatement: I'd heard their handful of singles to date on the radio ceaselessly, not to mention consistently having their CDs inflicted on me in my friends' cars throughout the course of my senior year of high school. I wasn't impressed. In fact, I found this Dave Matthews Band to be rather annoying. But I went to the show anyway, if for no other reason than for due diligence and to bring the monotonous hard sell of the band to an end once and for all.

Two minutes into the show and saxophonist LeRoi Moore's horn work on the opening song, "Seek Up," I was mesmerized. Never before had I seen *anything* like what this band was doing onstage. Dave Matthews was pouring his soul into the microphone, alternately expressing all of the anger, love, and humor I felt at that strange point in my life, which found me just on the cusp—in limbo somewhere between teenagehood and adulthood. Boyd Tinsley was otherworldly, his braids flying all around as he did things with a violin that I didn't know were possible, all the while with the hugest grin on his face I had ever seen. Bassist Stefan Lessard epitomized cool, laid-back grooviness, and drummer Carter Beauford's arms whirled about in an inconceivable way.

Despite the fact that I was in a major metropolitan sports complex with 19,599 other people dancing, screaming, singing, and swaying alongside me, there was a bizarre intimacy to it all. I knew I had found something that was *mine*. Not only did I feel as though I was completely at home (a feeling I rarely felt in those days), but for the first time I found a conduit that seemingly miraculously expressed all of the varied emotions that felt completely unique to myself at that point in life. I wasn't alone after all.

So it went from there. For months I buried myself in DMB, getting all of their studio albums, collecting as many recorded shows as I could, and immersing myself in the lyrics and alternately crazy and beautiful sounds. It was a process of discovery, and every day I found something new. On some days, "Drive In, Drive Out" seemed to concisely but completely express everything I was feeling; on others, it was "Cry Freedom," "Warehouse," or "Dancing Nancies." The whole process was a strange contrast of deeply personal and totally collective. Sometimes I would absorb the music on my headphones as I lost myself on the subway ride home or lying in bed listening to my stereo at night before going to sleep. At other times I shared the experience with my friends, who seemed to find the same solace, excitement, and hope in the music as I did. Together we'd alternate between listening in collective silence as incense burned and a joint was passed and enthusiastically discuss riffs and chords, rewinding tapes over and over again to listen to a part that grabbed us.

I became a junkie when it came to seeing DMB live, using my bi-coastal roots to my best advantage. If DMB was anywhere near New England (where I lived at the time) or the New York tri-state area, I was there; and if they were playing in California, well, that seemed like a good time for a trip home to see the family. I became a master of what I liked to call "multitasking."

As much as I fell in love with the band, I also fell in love with the crowd. It was the one place I could go that was completely contrary to everything I found in "real life." Everyone was happy and excited and welcoming. It was impossible not to make new friends, even for someone who was shy like me. Witnessing the band feed off the crowd and the crowd feed off the band was nothing short of euphoric—there was an understanding there, and I truly felt like part of something, perhaps for the first time ever. I chose to be there as much as the atmosphere chose me. Though I sometimes didn't know where I belonged in other areas of my life, I knew for sure that I belonged here at the shows, mismatched as the crowd sometimes was.

And so DMB became inextricable from my life. Every summer they played, and every summer I was there. No matter how broke I was, I could always find creative ways to scrape up money for the shows and the traveling they entailed. Sometimes I went with huge groups that would pile out of a rented bus or van and storm into venue parking lots en masse; other times I would enjoy a quiet night out with a single companion; and sometimes I would go alone, every time making new friends as I wandered around. Through the course of all this I saw the world—places I might never otherwise have seen, and that got into my blood too. It was all a big adventure, whether it was in the middle of New York City, in the most desolate reaches of Washington State, or amid the ancient splendor of Italy.

As is the case with many twenty-somethings, there weren't a lot of constants in my life at the time. But DMB—the shows, the atmosphere, the entire kit and caboodle—*that* was constant. And no matter where the shows were—even if it was somewhere completely foreign to me—they always felt like home.

Of course, no matter how successful or beloved, a band is still just a band, right? In some ways, yes. But although DMB has fans of all ages, shapes, and colors, many of us came of age or entered adulthood during a time in which devastating images of 9/11 were emblazoned in our heads; a time where society became increasingly more sterile seemingly overnight as e-mail, text messaging, and video games took the place of one-on-one interaction; a time during which trusting the government with our future often appeared a dubious strategy at best. Which all means that the escapes from reality that DMB provides—the happy, peaceful environment, the high-touch community, and the hopeful music and lyrics that celebrate one's ability to make a change and lead a fulfilling life—are important. They are a rare opportunity to indulge in all the things that are increasingly rare in the world today—a little taste of utopia and a glimpse of what could be if things were slightly different. If, maybe, things were a little bit better. And, on top of that, it was *fun*.

Over the course of the years, I learned that there were a lot of people out there like me. People who had their own stories, some quite similar to mine and others very different. People who felt the same way about DMB and the entire experience as I did. Oral history is very much alive among the DMB set. We like to share our stories: where we've been, what we've seen and heard, and how we got here. That's the weird thing about all of this; it's simultaneously completely personal and totally collective.

After being steeped in this culture and all these stories for well over a decade, it finally hit me as I found myself in the midst of a particularly nostalgic crowd at Berkeley's Greek Theatre in September 2008. As often tends to be the case in the world of DMB, this was an auspicious weekend. The three-night Berkeley stand marked the end of the band's 2008 tour, a tour that began wonderfully but ended tragically when founding member and saxophonist LeRoi Moore died suddenly following complications from an ATV accident. The band soldiered through the final remaining weeks of the tour following Moore's death, and it ended here, at the Greek, with the final show of the summer falling on what would have been the saxophonist's forty-seventh birthday. The last time the band had played this intimate theater thirteen years before, it had paid tribute to the recently deceased Jerry Garcia. This weekend we all gathered here again, this time to pay tribute to one of our own. Among the crowd, the scenario triggered a sudden rippling awareness of how precious and, perhaps, tenuous our situation really was. Hey, if the Deadhead experience could come to a screeching halt in the blink of an eye, it could certainly happen to us as well. So, that particular weekend, fans' stories ran rampant—remembering, sharing, and articulating what it all meant to us. It was on that weekend that I realized we didn't need anyone to explain the story of DMB to us. We could tell it ourselves, better than anyone else . . . because we were there. We've always been there.

So three years later, this is the story of DMB's first twenty years, as told by a collection of voices. Some of them have been around from the beginning, some since somewhere in the middle, and some for just a short while.

Although I shouldn't admit it (and especially here), in many ways words will never do this story justice. You can't really understand it unless you've been there, swaying to the music under the stars, with 19,999 friends by your side, all of whom are just as swept up as you are in the magic that begins onstage and filters out into the venue. But, with that in mind, this is nonetheless an attempt at putting all of those elusive commodities into words and explaining what exactly it is that keeps those hundreds of thousands of us coming back for more year after year after year.

—Nikki Van Noy

CHAPTER 1

AN EVENING SPENT DANCING

IT'S YOU AND ME

I t's just after 8:30 P.M. on November 20, 2010. As each minute ticks by, an excited sort of tension builds among the crowd that has gathered here at University of Virginia's John Paul Jones Arena in Charlottesville, Virginia. A collective, palpable buzz fills the air; it's so intense that it almost feels as though it's a tangible thing—as though you could reach out and touch the energy. As always, the DMB crowd is a tireless one. Spirits are high, despite the fact that some of the fans in the arena tonight have been camped out in the crisp, fall Charlottesville air since the end of the previous nights' show in an effort to get as close to the stage as possible.

The 16,000 fans who managed to grab one of the hot tickets for the sold-out show tonight have traveled from all over—from as far as California, Vermont, Alaska, even overseas from South America, the United Kingdom, and Portugal—because this is not just any show. Tonight marks Dave

Matthews Band's 1,797th performance, the concert that will effectively wrap up the first twenty years of the band's story. This particular tale is one that is at times beautiful, at other times tragic . . . but most of all, unlikely. In fact, "unlikely" is, in a nutshell, a large part of the DMB allure, which has enthralled millions of fans worldwide for the past two decades. Fittingly, in many ways, this milestone show finds the band just a couple miles away from where it all started. And although the venue has grown, the crowd has multiplied, and even some of the faces onstage have changed in the twenty years since DMB played its first show in this very same town, much has also remained the same.

Despite Dave Matthews Band's twenty-year career and the fact that many of the people in the audience tonight have seen it play dozens (if not hundreds) of times before, there is a sense of awe among the crowd (and among the band members themselves) as the group takes the stage. There are no sophisticated rock 'n' roll pyrotechnics or platforms harkening their arrival; the band members simply stroll out from stage left and meander toward their respective instruments under the dimmed stage lights, shadowy figures waving and peering out at the crowd as they go.

For its part, the audience has risen up into one giant roar; the thundering sound of screaming voices and stomping feet ricochets back and forth from one end of the arena to the other. For several distended moments, the band and audience take one another in. The audience continues to spin itself into a fever pitch, with hundreds of cat calls and requests swirling together, mingling in the smoky air. As the band gathers, for a moment the crowd comes together in unison, chanting "DMB!" at the top of their lungs.

The band members chatter and chuckle among themselves, responding to the occasional audience member, pointing at signs in the crowd, and generally taking it all in. They have already played before more than a million people across the United States, Europe, and South America over the course of this year alone, but this show is different, and everyone on stage and in the audience knows it. Front man and guitarist Dave Matthews saunters back and forth, pacing the stage and looking out at the audience as he sips from his always-present thermos of tea; when he raises his arms up high over his head in a victory motion, the crowd responds by turning the volume up even louder. Stefan Lessard rocks back and forth with his bass in hand, clearly revving himself up for what's about to come. They've performed this preconcert warm-up ritual thousands of times before, but there's definitely a special energy in the arena tonight. Not only is the adulation clear, it's obviously mutual.

After several minutes, nearly inaudible string plucks float off the stage and then suddenly take form as the opening notes of the song "You Might Die Trying" fill the air—at first soft and meandering, and then coming together in a booming full-band crescendo. All at once, the bass beats seem to form an invisible wall, hitting fans on the floor of the arena in the chest with their intensity. As the gigantic video screens and stage lights burst to life, casting a swirling purple and blue hue over the band, Dave's eyes sweep over the crowd while they gleefully shout out the chorus with him, pumping their fists in the air: "You might die trying!" As always, the audience is right there with him, singing at the top of their lungs, creating a gigantic, 16,000-person sing-along.

Like every other night, drummer Carter Beauford is wearing a signature jersey, but tonight it sports the number "91" on the front as an ode to the band's first year of existence, 1991. Carter peeks out from behind his enormous drum kit, grinning widely and casually blowing his bubble gum, as though moving his arms at the speed of light is the most natural thing in the world. Stefan Lessard stomps out the rhythm on his bass as he surveys the audience, a wide smile on his face. Violinist Boyd Tinsley steps forward between the chorus and the second verse and begins swiping at his fiddle, braids flying and face stretched in an ear-to-ear grin. On the electric guitar, touring member Tim Reynolds's notes seem to be singing along with Dave. Touring horn men Rashawn Ross and Jeff Coffin raise their trumpet and sax to their lips in unison. The Dave Matthews Band (DMB to the diehards in the audience) moves and plays as a single unit, the music unbelievably tight after months of touring throughout the course of 2010. Matthews's legs flail wildly as he turns to grin back at his bandmates and the crowd follows his lead, spasmodic dancing filling the Charlottesville arena. Generally speaking, but tonight especially, it's nearly impossible to believe that a band this seasoned maintains the ability to deliver energy so raw and intense that it actually seems to permeate the crowd and carry them away.

Though most major acts do not tour on an annual basis, over the past twenty years DMB has established a touring schedule that rivals that of any other act on the road today. Every single summer the band comes out to play, and every single summer their audience follows it from coast to coast, from Saratoga Springs, New York, to George, Washington. For DMB and its fans, summertime has evolved into a tradition of travel and community, with music at the core of it all. But tonight, with the announcement that the band will take a year off in 2011, an air of wistfulness hangs over the crowd. Both band and fans know that this is presumably the last time they will meet until the summer of 2012—an unprecedented hiatus in this little world. So tonight, the fans in John Paul Jones Arena are drowning themselves in the driving fiddle of "Dancing Nancies," the familiar and much-welcomed melodic drum and flute intro to "Say Goodbye," and the raging howls of a bluesy new rendition of "What You Are."

The road to this milestone moment has been a long and winding one, one that DMB and its fans have walked together hand in hand. Emerging on the music scene at the same time as bands such as Nirvana, Soundgarden, Smashing Pumpkins, and Counting Crows in the early 1990s, Dave Matthews was an unlikely band leader who seemed out of step with the grungy, low-fi sound of the era. This was only exacerbated by the band's unique and unclassifiable sound, with lush melodies and a heavy emphasis on horns and violin. There's no doubt that DMB was an unlikely candidate for mainstream music success. But from their early days playing the small bars and clubs of Charlottesville, the Dave Matthews Band has had a special and profound connection to its fans. The band knows it owes a portion of its ongoing success—in the years of top-40 domination as well as some of the more trying years of the 2000s—to the devoted fans who turn up again and again to see them play. Now, twenty years later, the Dave Matthews Band is that rarest of rare creatures in the music industry: a hugely successful band that has stood the test of time.

Seven studio albums, fifty-five official live releases (fifteen of which have been certified gold by the RIAA), and more than thirty million albums sold later, DMB has not only survived two decades in a fickle industry but has prospered. Though other bands may receive more consistent media attention or radio airtime, DMB has continued to climb the rungs of the music industry ladder in the background, taking its unlikely sound from the small clubs and bars of Virginia to an audience of 120,000 on Central Park's Great Lawn. They have shared the stage with some of the most legendary musicians and groups in the business today, including Neil Young, Santana, the Allman Brothers, and the Rolling Stones. This sustained effort has ultimately resulted in five consecutive number one debuts on the *Billboard* 200 (a feat that has been matched only by Jay-Z, Metallica, and DMX), Grammy nods, and the title of the number one live music act of the 2000s, with a gross of $530 million earned between 2000 and 2009 as determined by *Pollstar*.

This mainstream success grew from the most grassroots of efforts. Coming up in the small town of Charlottesville, DMB didn't exactly have easy access to movers and shakers in the music industry. Even if they had, its fusion of rock, jazz, world, rhythm, jam, and pop was a bit too off the beaten track for the music scene of the early 1990s. Even the DMB fans who were won over in the early days often describe their first reaction to the band's sound in one word: strange.

But combined with the band's intense yet buoyant energy and the celebratory vibe of its live show (which, according to early fans, was almost as much of a draw as the music itself), that very "strangeness" reeled people into DMB's first performances. Without these early fans, DMB might never have made its way very far outside those Virginia clubs—or, if it had, the scene that has grown around DMB would probably look much different than it does today. In 1991, just a few months into DMB's professional career, "tapers" came on the scene to document the band's sound, as crowds quickly realized that no two DMB shows were the same. The recordings they made spread throughout college campuses outside Virginia, so that even those who hadn't seen the band play became familiar with their sound. Whether through attendance at live shows or Memorex recordings, fans quickly latched onto this eclectic band as it made its way through bars and college campus venues throughout the southern states and eastern seaboard in its little red van. It was through these shows and recordings that the music spread slowly but surely from one campus to the next throughout the early 1990s.

And so it has continued. DMB still shows up like clockwork every summer, as do its fans. Thanks to improved technology, show recordings spread more quickly as each year goes by, and new fans come calling, joining the myriad that have now turned DMB into a virtual lifestyle. All the while, the band and music have continued evolving from the sparse and meandering acoustic sounds of *Under the Table and Dreaming* (1994) to the brash, more aggressive beats of *Big Whiskey and the GrooGrux King* (2009).

Over the years, DMB has experienced equal parts acclaim—for

albums such as *Crash* (1996) and *Before These Crowded Streets* (1998)—and criticism—*Everyday* (2001) and *Stand Up* (2005)—from critics and fans alike. Despite the band's successes, there have been plenty of obstacles to overcome along the way. By various members' own admission, the creatively trying times that lingered over the band in the early 2000s nearly led to their demise. And tragically, once things were back on track in 2008, DMB suddenly lost its founding member and saxophonist, LeRoi Moore, following a freak ATV accident.

But ultimately, even in the darkest of times, the story of DMB is not just a story about the band itself—it's also a story about a legion of fans who are among the most loyal and rabid of any in the music industry today. These fans feel a sense of *ownership* in the band and its music; it's a strangely proprietary relationship. Being a DMB fan is an active pursuit. It's not just about sitting around and listening to the music, it's about sharing music, traveling, and playing a part in a lively and energetic community. As Matt Yette, a cofounder of the DMB fan site antsmarching.org, puts it, "Basically, DMB is the modern-day Grateful Dead in terms of grassroots support."

For twenty years now, DMB concerts have been a staple of these fans' lives. For some, it's one show a summer at their local venue. For others, it's a matter of cramming in as many shows in as many places as possible over the course of the approximately four months per year that constitute an average DMB tour. In either case, shows have evolved into a tradition both for the band itself and for their fans. As the years have gone on, the live shows have become about much more than just music; they're a chance to visit both new and familiar spots, far-flung across the country (and, in some cases, the world) and to meet up with fellow fans who, over the years, have become lifelong friends with the shared appreciation of DMB's music at the friendship's core.

Many observers have likened DMB's appeal to that of bands like the

Grateful Dead and Phish. The comparisons are not totally unfounded—each has a group of music fans who are loyal and dedicated in their pursuit of live music and a robust touring culture supported by show taping and tune sharing. But DMB has garnered a unique cross-pollination of mainstream and cultlike attention. DMB is big enough that most radio listeners know hits like "Crash into Me" and "Ants Marching," even if they've never bought one of the band's albums or attended a show. On the other end of the spectrum, there are those who have memorized every single lyric of every single song (even those that have been played only in a sound-check setting), and made a lifestyle out of following the band. In many ways, it's the latter more cultlike following and not the mainstream success that really defines DMB and sets it apart from other major acts today. Indeed, the story of DMB is inextricable from the community that has grown around it. Over the years, this strange little band that refuses to be categorized has engendered an entire insular world that involves music, friendship, travel, and tradition.

And though many of life's most simple things are at the very core of DMB's message, there is also a complexity to the phenomenon. Coming onto the music scene around the time mainstream America began regularly accessing the Internet, DMB has found new and innovative ways to successfully navigate the quickly evolving and ever-changing music industry over the past twenty years, when even large, long-standing music labels have failed. In some cases, this technology has forced DMB to adapt and learn hard lessons—as was the case with the 2001 leak of *The Lillywhite Sessions,* an unfinished, unreleased album that spread like wildfire thanks to newly emerging Internet file-sharing and disc-burning capabilities.

But despite some bumps in the road, DMB has navigated the new digital landscape better than most bands, charting a path from the early-1990s heyday of the music industry to the more viral, crowd-driven scene of today. In many ways, technology has reinforced the sense of many fans that this band "belongs" to them, and over the past several years it has played an integral role in spreading the music and banding a community together. There is a striking dichotomy between the flat context of modern communication and the high-touch community this very mode of communication has fostered among members of the DMB fan base and, in some cases, the band members themselves. Ironically, in large part because DMB was the underdog and had to find its own way into the music scene in those earliest days, it has developed a flexibility and willingness to adapt and stay ahead of the curve.

Over the course of the past twenty years, plenty has been written about DMB. There have been books, thousands of articles in newspapers and magazines large and small, and millions of blogs and message board threads. But the real story of DMB lies in its fan base, which, over two decades' time, has banded together to form a community in the truest sense of the word. Like every other type of community, the DMB community is one with its own traditions, rituals, and history. This is a group of people that have been bonded together by music (and certainly it is music that will always be at its core) but from there has become so much more to so many people. Though there are certainly other bands with loyal followings, what makes the DMB fans so unique is that they have actually played an integral role in the trajectory of the band from day one. In so many ways, DMB fans are just as much a part of the story and history of this band as the musicians themselves. So, although much has already been written about this band, this is the story as told by the people who have witnessed it all go down and, more than that, played a large role in actually creating the story that is DMB.

The story of DMB is a story of technology and innovation. It's a story in which mainstream and cult dovetail. It's a story about passion and adventure. But, most of all, it's a love story about a band and its fans. Over the course of twenty years, this story has unfolded across a wide expanse including everything from tiny, obscure clubs and coffee shops in Virginia to some of the world's biggest stages.

Tonight that first chapter ends on the looming stage in John Paul Jones Arena. As the long, high-energy show creeps toward its end, a different sort of mania descends over the crowd. When the encore begins, it's clear that fans are not the only ones with misgivings about DMB's ensuing year off the road. Before launching into a solo version of "Some Devil," Dave addresses the audience, saying: "So, we're gonna take a little breather of some sort for a while, but it's not because I'm anything but the happiest and most blessed man, playing music with these people . . . I'm walking around tonight before we take this break thinking, What the hell am I doing, man?"

The band joins Dave once again for a satisfying rendition of one of its earliest songs, "Granny," and the audience goes crazy, with their shouts of "Love!" echoing throughout the arena. Next comes a "#40" tease, and finally (and appropriately), "The Last Stop." Emotion sweeps the audience as Dave softly sings the outro, interpolating Bob Marley's "Three Little Birds" and lingering on DMB's own lyrics—"For now good-bye . . . friend, good-bye."

After a booming crescendo, the band remains onstage for a while, waving at the audience and taking it all in for several moments. Both band and crowd seem hesitant to pull the curtain, and as the fans plant their feet down and refuse to let the night end, collectively chanting "One more song!," a discussion between Dave and Carter begins onstage. Though it's creeping toward midnight, curfew has passed, the soundboard has been shut down, and DMB has already played a long four-song encore, it appears that there's more to come. The band members who have already left the stage are summoned back. The crowd breaks into sheer pandemonium as DMB takes its time discussing what's to come. Suddenly, the stage lights flip back to life and the band bursts into a "Too Much" fake for a few seconds, before Stefan jumps to the front of the stage and begins rocking out with an "Anyone Seen the Bridge" bassline. Dave chimes in on acoustic, and then Rashawn and Jeff pitch in with a dramatic "Also Sprach Zarathustra" interpolation, straight out of *2001: A Space Odyssey*. The band is on fire as they quickly segue back into yet another "Too Much" fake, and then finally settle into the iconic "Ants Marching" to close the show. DMB and the crowd throw themselves into "Ants" with equal fervor, bidding one another a mutual adieu until 2012. Boyd takes it home, slithering across the front of the stage while playing a rocked out hoedown, all the while cheered on by the audience and fellow band members, who have formed a semi-circle, closing in on Carter's drum kit. As the audience loses its collective mind, Dave sings "Lights down, you up and die," marking the end of what is ostensibly the last song the band will play publicly until 2012. When the final note has been hit, the stage lights go up, but the band appears to be going nowhere soon, so intent are they on soaking up the crazed crowd before them. DMB remains onstage for several minutes as Carter throws out what seems to be dozens of drumsticks to a still uproarious audience, Dave stretches out to shake hands and slap high-fives with fans in the front few rows, and Boyd gazes out at the crowd, smiling, waving, and clapping right back at them, with his shades still firmly in place despite the darkness of the arena. Fittingly, in the final seconds before leaving the stage, Dave and Carter grab each other in a huge bear hug, leaving the audience with this final image of DMB. A few minutes after midnight, and the show is finally over once and for all. DMB has officially clocked the longest set they've played in recorded DMB history, with three hours and one minute worth of song time and a set list that has stretched a mile long. There's no doubt that even after all this time and all the miles they've logged, this is a band at the top of their game.

For all that has changed in twenty years' time, some things have remained constant all the way from the tiny bars the band played in its earlier years to the stadiums that marked the chaotic peak of their mainstream success in the late 1990s and early 2000s: DMB's music still defies you *not* to move, *not* to feel the energy, *not* to fall in love. And so it is that two decades after it all began, DMB and their faithful fans are still here dancing.

CHAPTER 2

GETTING STARTED

THINGS WERE QUIET THEN

Although DMB has come to represent much more than just music over the past twenty years, of course it all began with the music, and it's the music that remains the centerpiece today. It all started in the small but artistically vibrant town of Charlottesville, Virginia, nestled just outside Thomas Jefferson's famed residence, Monticello.

Made up of a diverse combination of members with a fifteen-year age spread and an eclectic combination of ethnic and musical backgrounds, DMB begins to make more sense once one understands the unique culture of the late 1980s in Charlottesville. In this town, the arts (and music, especially) transcend differences in age, ethnicity, and musical genre. It's not out of the ordinary to see a sixty-year-old blues horn player sitting in with a young, up-and-coming rock band or a twenty-year-old classically trained guitarist playing a set with a well-established jazz fusion band. A musician and then bartender at the local watering hole Eastern Standard, Mark Roebuck, remembers the Charlottesville scene of that era as being infused with "this remarkable vibe of cross-pollination of music. Every night we'd just gather at the bars until about five or six A.M. I'll never forget it. There was a lot of sparking of ideas and a lot of really varied types of music that were being created and discussed at the time."

David McNair, a writer and editor at Charlottesville's alt weekly *The Hook* and a part of the local bar and artistic circles Dave Matthews dwelled in during those pre-DMB days explains, "There was a lot of collaboration going on. I was sort of in the writers' circle, and that overlapped with what a lot of the musicians were doing. It also involved the restaurant and bar scenes too. There's a huge network of musicians here, and they were all connected to what was happening with DMB."

All it takes is a stroll through this lively college town to understand that music, the arts, and community are an integral part of life. On the Downtown Mall, strains of music flood through the air, pouring out of various cafés, clubs, and bars. On a warm day, this is intermingled with the sound of street musicians playing for the stream of people out and about, soaking in the atmosphere. And if you happen to walk down the strip on just the right day, all this is accompanied by larger acts playing at the Charlottesville Pavilion, a tented outdoor venue that borders the south end of the Downtown Mall.

Though even if today's Downtown Mall *does* provide an insightful glimpse into the genesis of DMB, McNair is quick to point out that the Charlottesville of today is not the same Charlottesville DMB found its roots in during the late 1980s and early '90s. "It seemed like it was a much smaller town back then, and there was a definite scene on the Downtown Mall. The Downtown Mall today is very populated—lots of stores, lots of restaurants. And it wasn't like that back then."

The journalist and editor Bill Ramsey, who penned a column titled "DMBeat" for the Charlottesville alt weeklies *C-Ville* and *The Hook*, describes the town as a unique artistic enclave. "Charlottesville is an oasis of sorts in Virginia—laid back but also very sophisticated with a vibrant art and music scene propelled by a very intelligent audience and, of course, the large student population of the University of Virginia (UVA). Rare is the week when you don't witness a great show or exhibit. It's sort of like a slice of Greenwich Village if it were plopped down in the Revolutionary War period. I think that—and the beautiful backdrop of the Blue Ridge Mountains, the rolling countryside, and, of course, the city's historic ambiance—is what attracts people such as John Grisham to live here. I certainly found it a magical place to live."

It was on the Downtown Mall of this pulsating town within the dark, nondescript confines of Miller's Downtown Restaurant that DMB found its roots. McNair describes Miller's place on the Charlottesville music scene of the time: "There was really one bar where everybody congregated, and that was Miller's. It was remote at the time. Not a lot of people from the university came down there. It was just a real sort of writers' and artists' hangout. Everybody knew one another."

In 1986, the South African-born Matthews followed his family back to Charlottesville after a brief stint in New York City, where Dave worked for IBM as a temporary clerk. Though Dave was born in South Africa, the Matthews family had Charlottesville roots dating back prior to Dave's birth, so their return to the area was a homecoming of sorts. Only nineteen years old when he relocated to Charlottesville, Matthews had already seen a lot of life. Following the death of his father, John Matthews, while the family was living in New York State when Dave was only ten years old, his mother moved Dave and his three siblings back to South Africa so they could be near her extended family. Because of this, Matthews came of age in a society where apartheid was rampant.

Raised in the Quaker tradition and staunchly antiapartheid, Dave left South Africa upon high school graduation in an effort to avoid the draft. Through his lyrics and political statements later in life, it's clear that the racially tense culture of his beloved native country had a profound effect on Dave and his worldview.

Once in Charlottesville, Matthews got a job at Miller's, working his way up the ranks from salad boy to server to bartender. While pulling drafts and pouring whiskeys, he began developing relationships with many of the local musicians who found their way into the bar, either to play music on a stage not much larger than the size of a bedroom closet or simply to have a few drinks and mingle. Included among these regulars were drummer Carter Beauford, saxophonist LeRoi Moore, and local guitar prodigy Tim Reynolds, all of whom were familiar faces on the local music circuit.

It was at Miller's that Matthews and Reynolds formed a friendship and frequently jammed together on guitar. Though Dave had begun playing guitar at age nine, he was primarily a "closet musician" until he met up with Tim; in fact, Matthews's first local performances were guest spots with Reynolds's band TR3. Although it's highly unlikely that anyone attended these random early shows specifically to see the then-unknown Dave Matthews play, according to Andy Garrigue, a former music critic for the Richmond, Virginia, publication *Style Weekly* and an employee at the indie Plan 9 Music, those shows would later become a source of local mythology. Because Matthews had not yet begun writing his own songs, he would perform covers, most notably Bob Marley's "Exodus." Garrigue remembers chatting with one Plan 9 customer who proudly boasted that he had once seen Dave play a forty-minute version of "Exodus" at Miller's.

Another prominent figure in the Charlottesville music and bar scene in the late 1980s was Mark Roebuck, the lead singer of the local power pop band the Deal and a bartender at the now-defunct Eastern Standard. Roebuck and the Deal had their own brush with fame in the early to mid-1980s when Warner Bros' Bearsville Records head Albert Grossman (who had previously managed major artists such as Bob Dylan, Janis Joplin, and Peter, Paul and Mary) signed them. Locally, great things were expected of the Deal, but the band's forward trajectory came to a screeching halt when Grossman suffered a fatal heart attack while on an airplane en route to London.

In the wake of the breakup of the Deal, Roebuck found himself "floating along on bartending work. I was working at the Eastern Standard, as were several members of the music group Pavement." Despite the bar's musical staff, Eastern Standard was not hosting any musical events of its own until Roebuck started open-mic nights as a way of bolstering business during his quiet Monday-night shifts. Dave became a frequent musician at those weekly showcases, often playing gigs with fellow Miller's employee and harmonica player and keyboardist Peter Griesar.

Roebuck remembers being impressed by Dave, despite his relatively new stature on the Charlottesville music scene. "I just really remember being struck by how original his guitar playing was and how I'd never really seen anyone play that quarter-note stuff and sing at the same time. I remember thinking he was just *wildly* original from the first time he played." According to Roebuck, he was not the only one impressed by Dave's unique guitar and vocal style. Roebuck fondly remembers receiving a phone call one Monday night when the Indigo Girls were playing at the local Trax nightclub. "It was open-mic night, and I got a phone call saying the Indigo Girls might consider coming down after their show. Well past the point it was legal to do so, I kept the bar open. The Indigo Girls came in and sang, and I remember Dave getting up and singing 'All Along the Watchtower' and just blowing them away." Roebuck laughs, "It was an extremely cool night that I could have gotten in a lot of trouble for."

Based on his knowledge of Matthews both from open-mic nights and through the more general bar scene, Roebuck decided to enlist the young up-and-comer's help in writing a couple of songs for some new projects he was working on. While they worked together on Roebuck's songs during that first writing session, Roebuck remembers Dave playing an unfinished song of his own. "I can remember when he came over to my house for the very first time, we sort of swapped stuff and he played a song that he said wasn't finished." Shortly thereafter, during another writing session in Matthews's mother's basement (where Dave was living at the time), Roebuck says he and Matthews together finished the lyrics. The end result, "The Song That Jane Likes," was Matthews's first completed song. (Completely unrelated to the lyrics of this song, this somewhat elusive title is a reference to Dave's sister, Jane, who, somewhat obviously, likes the song.) Though "The Song That Jane Likes" would go on to be included on the DMB album *Remember Two Things*, it was originally recorded with eight other tracks for the 1989 album demo *Imagine We Were*, which Dave and Mark recorded under the name Tribe of Heaven. Though record labels didn't pick up this demo when it was first shopped in 1990, it enjoyed a much-delayed release fifteen years later by the Fear of the Atom record label.

In many ways, it's fitting that it was Roebuck who helped Dave finish that first song. The local journalist David McNair can't help but draw some parallels between DMB and its Charlottesvillian musical ancestors the Deal. "It's interesting," McNair muses. "Nothing happens in a vacuum— that's what I've learned from all of this. DMB definitely had some influences, and one of them was the Deal. The Deal became successful in the same way DMB did: playing lots of college gigs on the East Coast. [Albert] Grossman was going to take them to the top, but it just sort of disintegrated after his death. But the members of the Deal were big influences on David, specifically Roebuck and his then bandmate Haines Fullerton. David made his first recording with Roebuck. And Haines was a great, great musician, a great guitarist, and a big influence on David—someone who kept encouraging him. He said, 'You're going to be famous.' He predicted a lot of things. And since Roebuck and Haines had kind of been there in a way, they were very influential for David and his band." (The now-deceased Haines Fullerton also went on to cowrite the DMB song "#34" with Dave, LeRoi Moore, and Carter Beauford as a tribute to a fellow Charlottesville musician, Miguel Valdez; "#34" was ultimately included on the DMB album *Under the Table and Dreaming*.)

It was with his recordings of "The Song That Jane Likes" and three other songs ("I'll Back You Up," "Recently," and "The Best of What's Around"), that Dave decided to approach two local musicians, the drummer Carter Beauford and the saxophonist LeRoi Moore, one night at Miller's to request that they accompany him on a second demo recording. Although Dave had by then become somewhat of a familiar face on the Charlottesville music circuit based on his performances at Eastern Standard open-mic nights and cameos with TR3, there is no doubt that Carter and LeRoi were far more accomplished, better-recognized musicians. When asked about the experience of approaching those two musicians in a 2009 interview with CBS's *Sunday Morning,* Matthews laughingly remembered, "I was really nervous, embarrassed—ashamed almost."

Carter Beauford, who would go on to be ranked fifteenth out of the hundred greatest drummers of all time by *Rolling Stone* in 2009, grew up surrounded by music. Carter's father was a professional trumpet player, and it was he who inadvertently introduced his three-year-old son to drumming by taking him to see the drummer Buddy Rich play. Despite the fact that he was practically a baby at the time, this would prove to be a pivotal moment in Carter's life. Seeing his son's excitement over Rich, Carter's father bought him a drum kit shortly after the concert, and thus a drumming career began. By the time he was nine years old, Beauford was drumming professionally with "Big Nick" Nicholas's fusion band. He supplemented his professional training with a formal education, receiving a degree from Virginia's Shenandoah Conservatory. Over the years, Carter became a familiar face on the Charlottesville and Richmond music scenes, playing with the local jazz groups Blue Indigo and Secrets, both of which his childhood friend and saxophonist LeRoi Moore was also a member. Carter also managed to step outside the local music scene to a broader national stage through his drum work on the cable television show *BET on Jazz.*

His fellow musician Mark Roebuck vividly remembers being awe-struck the first time he saw Beauford play. "I very much remember the first time I saw Carter and the band Secrets at a club called C&O. I was just blown away. He was just acknowledged to be *the* best well before he associated with Dave. I remember seeing him that first time and really not believing my ears—I couldn't fathom how tight and creative he was."

As with Beauford, music had been a part of LeRoi Moore's life since childhood, when he had begun playing alto sax in his Charlottesville junior high band. He had gone on to study tenor saxophone at James Madison University and from there had become a fixture on the Charlottesville music circuit. In addition to playing with Carter in Blue Indigo and Secrets, LeRoi also cofounded and played with the Charlottesville Swing Orchestra and collaborated with the well-known local trumpeter John D'earth in the John D'earth Quintet (which frequently played Miller's).

LeRoi made a big impact on then-bartender Dave Matthews at those Miller's gigs. Following the saxophonist's death in 2008, Dave reminisced, "I was at this bar in Virginia and, on a rare occasion, Roi liked to drink a bit. I remember that he'd had quite a bit and the stage was right near the cash register, so he just went over to the cash register because it had a counter and he [leaned] on it because standing had become somewhat of a chore. And he played the most beautiful version of 'Somewhere over the Rainbow' I ever heard in my whole life. That's the day I fell in love with him, and I still love him."

His comparative novice stature aside, Dave was nonetheless able to convince Carter and LeRoi to help him lay down those first four songs. Although it's impossible to know what ultimately persuaded the two more veteran musicians to join the project, Mark Roebuck explains Matthews's style as compelling, despite his comparative lack of experience. "I just never heard anyone play like him. I was privy to a lot of the early songs as they were being written, and from the beginning the patterns he would do while singing, I've never heard anyone else do."

But even so, David McNair explains, the collaboration of Matthews, Beauford, and Moore was unlikely. "Each one of the members was an individual performer here. It's interesting because everyone except Dave had been in town for a while. The rest had made a name for themselves locally. You'd think that their chances of something like this happening were over because they were sort of older at the time; except for David, they weren't spring chickens. The question mark was Dave. It took guts for him to go up to these guys who were established, well-respected musicians and say, 'Hey, do you wanna start a band?' I think all of them were a bit skeptical at first, because I don't think that Dave had much experience. But they were quickly charmed by him, noticed his charisma, and got involved."

According to McNair, Matthews's unique charisma may well have compensated for what he then lacked in musical experience, both for the initial band members and for the band's earliest crowds. "He was a little strange in the early days. He had really, really long hair down to his butt. I don't think a lot of people knew what to make of him. But he was very charming. Early on, even before the band, girls were, like, 'Hey, there's a cute bartender at Miller's.' He had that charm early on. But most of all, he's just a *great* guy. And always has been, through the whole thing—always the same guy. He just pours himself into what he does in an open, exploring, kind of tense, loving sort of way."

For Roebuck's part, the biggest surprise about the collaboration was not that Carter and LeRoi would partner with a less experienced musician such as Dave but that LeRoi was compelled by Dave's more acoustically driven folk-rock style of music. "I associated [LeRoi] as a very, very deep jazz character, and when he first started playing with Dave it took me by surprise. I thought of LeRoi as a sort of modern-day Charlie Parker, just completely committed to jazz. It was surprising to me when he was added to the lineup."

Together, Dave, Carter, and LeRoi began fiddling with the songs Matthews had written, rehearsing alternately in Carter's mom's basement and Dave's mom's basement. According to both Beauford and Matthews, it wasn't exactly instantaneous magic. Of these earliest practice sessions, Beauford told Charlie Rose in 2000, "When we started out, it was a scary thing. It sounded like absolute crap. It sounded terrible, it was the worst thing I've ever heard in my life." Though Matthews didn't disagree, in the same interview he told Rose that he *did* sense that there was something there, despite the fact that their music wasn't exactly melding. "I think the first time we got together and started to play, there must have been a magic in there. Even if we were a bit shocked about what was going on and how horrible it was, we must have said, 'Wow, there's something here in how our personalities all mix and how our music mixes.'"

Deciding they needed a fuller sound, the trio added a fourth musician to round out the recordings just a couple of rehearsals in. Despite his young age, then-sixteen-year-old bass player Stefan Lessard had already begun to build a reputation for himself through his work with the Charlottesville trumpeter and frequent Miller's musician John D'earth, who taught Stefan at the Tandem Friends School. As the youngest member of DMB, Stefan was playing bars and clubs before he could even legally get into them. Although DMB ultimately proved to be a happy accident for Lessard, it was in many ways exactly that—an accident.

Early on, Stefan was forced to decide between the band's heavy touring schedule and continuing his education at Virginia Commonwealth University. Stefan remembers, "I wanted to go to school and be a band leader. I wanted to write music and have ensembles and orchestras play it. I was going 'Rock Me Amadeus'-style. And now I'm the bass player in a really popular band. It wasn't in my sights when I was a teenager. I just sort of fell into it. But the chance to work with professional musicians—I always believed you never turn that down. So the opportunity to work with Carter and to work with LeRoi and to work with Dave, how can you turn that down? How can I not do that when that's available to me now?"

Although today it's all but impossible to imagine a Dave Matthews Band without the unique fiddle sound that has come to characterize staple songs such as "Ants Marching," "Dancing Nancies," and "Lie in Our Graves," the band spent its first few months of existence sans Boyd Tinsley. It was not until DMB went to lay down the demo track for "Tripping Billies" in February 1991 that LeRoi Moore suggested it add a fiddle to color the recording's sound. The obvious choice was the Charlottesville-based fiddle player Boyd Tinsley, who was known locally for his work with the Boyd Tinsley Band and Down Boy Down.

Like Carter and LeRoi, Boyd had been a musician for the greater part of his life, stumbling upon the violin accidentally in middle school when he signed up for a strings class under the mistaken assumption that he would learn guitar. Though it was actually an orchestra class, Boyd continued on, sticking with classical violin. Tinsley redirected his orchestral musical direction around the time he attended the University of Virginia as an undergraduate and began collaborating with musicians who were playing more modern rock music. This unique melding of violin with traditional rock instruments was the signature sound of his work with both the Boyd Tinsley Band and the two-man band Down Boy Down.

In addition to being a known commodity among local musicians, Boyd had somewhat of a presence on the UVA campus. The then UVA undergraduate David Leshner remembers, "Boyd would play with Down Boy Down at fraternities. I actually saw him play before I had any idea who Dave Matthews was." Though Boyd maintained the Boyd Tinsley Band after recording the initial "Tripping Billies" demo, it led to several sit-in gigs with DMB, and in April 1992 Boyd officially joined DMB full-time.

Despite the fact that the band was originally put into place for the sole purpose of laying down demo recordings of Dave's four songs, its members meshed well enough that they decided to begin playing live performances together. For years, common knowledge held that DMB had made its debut performance on April 20, 1991, at the Earth Day Festival in Charlottesville's Meade Park. However, nearly two decades later, in October 2010, Stefan Lessard surprised the DMB community by announcing via Twitter that he had found a tape that established that the band actually made their first public appearance more than a month before that, with a seven-song set as part of a benefit show at Charlottesville's Trax on March 14, 1991. It should be noted that this initial Trax outing consisted only of Dave, Stefan, Carter, and LeRoi. The final founding member of DMB, Boyd Tinsley, did not appear until the April 20 Meade Park show, making that the first time all five members of DMB appeared publicly onstage together. That was followed shortly thereafter by a May 11, 1991, performance on the rooftop of the South Street Warehouse, located just a couple blocks away from the Downtown Mall. (Although the venue was innocuous at the time, it has gone on to achieve great fame among DMB fans thanks to the song "Warehouse," which appears on the band's *Under the Table and Dreaming* album.)

In August 1991, the final DMB-Miller's connection came in the form of the keyboardist and harmonica player Peter Griesar, who rounded out the band's original lineup. Also employed by Miller's, Peter made a name for himself on the Charlottesville music scene by way of the group the Basics, of which LeRoi Moore and guitarist Tim Reynolds were also members. When DMB was allowed to use Miller's for practice space during the bar's renovations in August 1991, Peter jammed with them on harmonica and was immediately brought on board to play keyboards and harmonica. Although Griesar played his last DMB show at Trax on March 23, 1993, his mark on the band can still be seen through the legacy of the song "So Much to Say," which he cowrote with Dave and Boyd. This tune is still considered typical of the quintessential DMB sound, with its distinct acoustic guitar, driving rhythm, bellowing sax, and full-band crescendo, all underlying whimsical yet introspective lyrics.

Also notably in August 1991, DMB was booked by Mark Roebuck to play its first series of regularly paid shows at Eastern Standard. The gig paid fifty dollars, and drinks were on the house. A handful of Tuesday-night shows at Eastern Standard, which Roebuck recalls as "wildly successful," followed throughout the remainder of 1991. Roebuck says, "They started getting crowds fast, so I didn't have the luxury of watching them play too much because I was making drinks, but I liked their sound." Roebuck attributes DMB's almost instantaneous local draw to the fact that "David had become a pretty beloved character on the Downtown Mall. When he played by himself at open-mic nights, he impressed people, so he already had sort of a fan base. The other guys had such reputations that I think people just really wanted to see this band."

A smattering of shows throughout Charlottesville at random venues followed before the band began making regular appearances at the now-defunct (and legendary to DMB fans) 900-capacity venue Trax, a Charlottesville music venue located a few blocks from UVA on West Main Street, on August 31, 1991. Trax's mixed crowd drew both those who were into the local music scene and a healthy stream of UVA students. Then a student at UVA who frequented DMB's Trax shows, David Leshner

remembers the venue as fairly bare bones. "It was just a Spartan building with not much on the inside. It was definitely not like a nightclub or
a luxurious venue. It had a warehouse feeling to it. There was a bar there
and just a big, open space for music. Not at all like any sort of fancy stadium or club. It was definitely a place where you just went to see music
and hang out."

DMB quickly became a Trax staple, and before long its shows were
a recurring weekly event—every Tuesday night, the band would play to an
ever-growing crowd at Trax. It was also here that the band hooked up with
Trax's owner, Coran Capshaw, who would go on to manage the band and
found Red Light Management, which continues to oversee DMB to this day.
Andy Garrigue, who conducted several interviews with various band members and Capshaw as well over the course of the 1990s for Plan 9 Music's
9x online publication and Richmond's *Style Weekly,* believes that Capshaw
has been a critical key to DMB's success. "He told me some spark hit him
and he just really wanted to work with this band so badly, he started out
working pro bono for a while. Coran explained he absolutely had a strategy
to go to certain markets and play repetitively so the audience could de-
pend on DMB being there. Someone sees DMB once and thinks, 'They're
okay,' twice and they're hooked, the third time they bring one friend, the
fourth time twenty friends."

Even in the band's infancy, many of the qualities that have drawn two
decades' worth of audiences from far and wide to show after show after
show were apparent. "There was such a sense of joy and celebration about
it all," David McNair remembers of the Trax shows. "You just went to those
Tuesday-night gigs because they were so great. There was a feeling there.
And I think people recognized *that* before they attached any importance
to the band. Some people probably went there and didn't even know the
names of the guys in the band. It was more like 'Wow, they're really good.'
We weren't thinking of them as big stars. You looked forward to those

Tuesday-night performances, and you'd always end up having a good time. There was a great sort of mood and enthusiasm. It's probably similar to the reasons people follow them around today. It was a feeling and a *gathering,* and the scene was different than anything else out there. It wasn't like sitting there and listening to a metal band or dark music. It just made you feel so buoyant and joyous."

Because of its close proximity to campus, DMB's regular Trax shows offered UVA students the perfect setting to blow off steam and enjoy a few beers every Tuesday night. With the booming music scene in Charlottesville and the reputations of the DMB players, of course other people were attending the shows as well, but the high percentage of UVA students effectively meant that a network of sorts was in place from the very beginning. Bill Lakenan, who began taping DMB's shows while it was still a relatively regional act, remembers, "There was a sort of hippie, free spirit that could be had. Not to the extent of Dead shows, but in the early days at the back of the room there were always people dancing around, twirling, looking down at their dresses, really enjoying the vibe." As is the case on most college campuses, word of mouth about the band spread quickly throughout the student network at UVA, and DMB's weekly draw at Trax became larger and larger as each week passed.

With its Charlottesville audience quickly and easily secured, the band started to branch out to nearby areas. Beginning in May 1992, DMB also picked up weekly Wednesday-night gigs at the Flood Zone in Richmond, Virginia, just over an hour away from Charlottesville and also owned by Coran Capshaw. One fan, Steven Boyette, remembers the ritual of weekly five-dollar Wednesday-night shows at the Flood Zone fondly. "I worked at a restaurant in [nearby] Williamsburg at the time," Boyette reflects. "I always had a line drawn through my schedule on Wednesday nights, and everybody knew there was no way I was switching shifts with them to work a Wednesday—that's when I saw DMB."

Although it's now defunct, the Flood Zone still holds a fond place in the minds of music fans like Boyette. "It was a cool place, a converted warehouse. The ground floor was sort of rectangular with a bar on one side of it. Then you could go upstairs to the second floor, which was a U shape. You could walk all the way along the U until you were basically standing on top of the stage. I spent a lot of time up there watching Carter, but I'd also go down to the floor and dance. You could set your beer on the stage, go to the bathroom, come back and pick up your beer. That's how loose it was there."

A witness to the phenomenon since 1991, Mark Lynn, watched the Flood Zone DMB scene explode before his eyes. "In early 1992 you could go catch a show at Flood Zone and there were only fifteen or twenty people there. But by December of that year, it was packed to the rafters."

The journalist Andy Garrigue remembers experiencing a similar sense of shock at how quickly the phenomenon developed. Having heard about DMB through word of mouth in Richmond, he decided to go check out one of its weekly Wednesday gigs for a write-up on *Style Weekly* on-line. "I got down there around 9:30 P.M. and was expecting there would be a couple hundred kids from University of Richmond and that it would be really happening. I walked into Flood Zone, and there were literally only a handful of people there for the show and a few more people sitting up in the merch booths, complete with a dog under the merch table. It was really low-key—actually, really *dead* is a better word for it. I stood around for five or ten minutes, then decided to leave and just cruise around for a half hour. When I came back I couldn't believe it, because there had to be at least five hundred people in there—I was only gone for thirty minutes, not a significant amount of time. It was very full and very lively. There was lots of excitement in the air. I remember thinking, 'Wow! This audience is trained.'"

Well versed in the Richmond music scene at the time, Garrigue explains that DMB's draw was not only impressive but also extremely atypical: "I had covered Richmond for a few years before that show and for many years after it, and I know how hard it is to draw a crowd of even a hundred people, even when you're getting press from multiple sources and you've been doing it for twenty years. I've been embarrassed by the low turnout for some fabulous acts, and this was just a Wednesday night at ten P.M. Here's a band from out of town that can draw five hundred people in a town where it's hard to draw a hundred—and not only that, but the audience is showing up like clockwork." Garrigue attributes this abnormally large and consistent draw to a combination of quality musicianship and determination. "First of all, people knew about them and liked them. Friends were telling friends, 'Hey, you gotta come check this band out.' I just felt like DMB managed to inform people about themselves based on grassroots marketing, as it were, by way of consistent shows with a very low cover charge or no cover at all. And then the music just spread because it was infectious, high-quality music. It seemed to be a sound that people really liked."

Then a law student at University of Richmond, Shannon Kearns describes the Charlottesville and Richmond scenes as quite different, despite their close proximity. "Charlottesville was more of a typical college scene, whereas Richmond was a bigger city and more diverse. Because of that, DMB's crowds in Richmond were more diverse too." Flood Zone regular Steven Boyette concurs. "Richmond definitely pulled more of a mixed crowd. The Flood Zone wasn't just dominated by a young crowd. There were people there who had gotten word on the street and were probably in their midthirties. You had an eclectic group of young twenty-somethings to midthirty-somethings at that time."

Though, by all accounts, Trax turned into a bit of a madhouse at times, Shannon Kearns remembers the early Richmond DMB scene as generally being much more relaxed. "When I saw them at Browns Island [an island in Richmond where outdoor concerts are held], people were just casually walking into the area. It was just a very calm, spread-out, kickback crowd. People were just milling around. They weren't worried about getting up close to the stage or getting in the front row. They were just hanging out."

The draw of "hanging out" at DMB shows cannot be overstated. From early on, it was about more than just the music. Bill Lakenan remembers that even in the early days, the small community was a big draw to the DMB shows. "I got exposed to the scene and really pulled in because I started taping. It was really tight—everybody knew everybody. It was much more of the scene than the music that I got pulled into."

Ironically for a band that had originally been formed for the sole purpose of recording in the studio, DMB was quickly growing into a compelling live act that, in the absence of an officially released album, existed solely as an onstage entity. Though set lists from the earliest days of 1991 and 1992 are somewhat difficult to come by, fans attest that the music changed from night to night and new songs (both originals and cover songs) were frequently added to the band's repertoire.

Despite the band's somewhat misleading eponymous moniker (which came to be only as a spur-of-the-moment reaction when the members were asked for a band name for booking purposes), DMB was, indeed, a collaborative effort in every way. Based on interviews with the band and his impressions of it live, Andy Garrigue comments, "I thought the band was really strong and Dave worked well within the band. I didn't see him as this front guy that was totally leading things. It definitely seemed like a group thing where all members were equal. When I asked him about the creative process, Dave said he might have a kernel of something and Stefan would add a bass line and Carter would add the rhythm. Dave was adamant that it was truly collaborative; maybe two people would head something up, but it was all of the members getting in on it."

In some ways, early audiences were bought into this collaborative song-building effort as well. It would appear that, as creative as DMB was at actually writing songs, coming up with titles for them was a different story. This is clearly evidenced by some songs titles (such as "#34," "#36," "#40," and "#41"), which derive their names simply from the chronological order in which they were written. (This orderly chronological titling system did not last for the duration of the band's career. For example, "#27"—which, according to antsmarching.org was actually the 133rd song written by DMB—is haphazardly numbered and named.) Matthews references this involvement and asked the crowd to help come up with a name for the then-untitled song "Heathcliff's Haiku Warriors" at the March 23, 1993, show, saying "This is a brand-new song, it has no name. And again the old request: if you hear any words that you like, please write them down and tell them to our soundman there in the back. Thank you very much."

With this collaborative effort, DMB quickly put itself into a position where it had enough songs to mix up the rotation on a night-to-night basis. Combined with the band's ability to improvise and jam onstage, even early audiences were sure to see a different show every night—an essential part of the allure of a band that was frequenting a small number of venues in close proximity to one another. Also, because songs had not yet been committed to recordings, lyrics were constantly in flux and in-progress songs would change from night to night. Combined with Matthews's rambling onstage mutterings—later termed "Davespeak" and a continual source of amusement for fans; over the years Dave's offbeat commentary has run the gamut from observations about monkeys to anecdotes about his own personal drunken antics—fans truly never knew what to expect on any given night.

Not only did organic set lists keep things fresh, they also gave DMB's emerging fan base something to talk and speculate about. Steven Boyette remembers that such conversations with regulars at Flood Zone were part of the band's allure. "There were people that we saw every week, that we became friends with. Aside from the music, that was something that struck me—the culture. Because the band was constantly changing up set lists, there was always that anticipation of 'What are we going to hear tonight?' to keep us regulars bonded and keep the conversation flowing. Which was really, really cool and definitely something that helped keep me interested."

As much of a draw as the scene was to those who witnessed Trax and Flood Zone shows, without the benefit of an album to spread their reputation, DMB's appeal could well have remained limited to the close confines of the Charlottesville and Richmond areas. By all accounts, word of mouth about the potential of the newly formed Dave Matthews Band spread throughout Charlottesville almost instantaneously. But no matter how much local momentum existed, chances are that if history had been written slightly differently, DMB might have never hit the national music scene in such a massive way—or at all, for that matter. The band bucked many of the musical trends of the time and, by its own admission, initially had a difficult time breaking through to big stages and record labels. And in the early 1990s, without the benefit of national visibility or airtime, there were few other outlets through which to make one's music known.

Luckily for DMB, though, from very early on fans took matters in their own hands. A DMB taper since 1992, Richmond native Mark Lynn explains, "At the time, taping was a big thing in the area. People used to joke that you received a microphone along with your mortgage here." And so it was that fans like Lynn didn't think twice about taking their mics to DMB's early club shows. It was just what they did.

Steven Boyette remembers, "We were bringing our home cassette players. Literally, we'd haul in the big, black, rectangular box from our stack stereos at home." But in those early days before DMB had released a CD, Boyette remembers that even the lower-quality tapes served a great purpose. "We'd have an hour-and-fifteen-minute drive home from the

Flood Zone and could listen to the show on the car's cassette deck on the way home. Which at that point in time was a great novelty—we couldn't instantaneously get live music like we can now. To be able to watch the show, then ride home and listen to the same show in the car—to me, I *was* twenty-first century at that point."

The first known existing tape is from August 21, 1991 (a four-song set at Eastern Standard in Charlottesville), just four months after the band's first show and early enough that Peter Griesar and Boyd Tinsley had not yet started playing with DMB (although Boyd was a guest on this particular night). In hindsight, the allowance of taping was a brilliant tactical move on the part of DMB and its management, but taper Mark Lynn's impression at the time was that it was really a fortuitous accident. "Everyone knew that Coran was a Deadhead and, because of that, presumably understood the taping culture. But at the time, it didn't seem orchestrated or like a grassroots marketing ploy at all. We just sort of brought our equipment with us, and they shrugged their shoulders and let us use it. I'm not even sure that all of the band members knew we were taping at first."

Whether the whole taping scene was ultimately accidental or not, the DMB fan site antsmarching.org cofounder Matt Yette reflects, "I think Coran did a good job because he got out of the way of taping. I think if he had tried to control and force and manipulate it, it never would have gone down like this." So agreeable was the band to taping that in those first years DMB soundman Jeff "Bagby" Thomas allowed tapers to plug into the actual DMB sound board. In recognition of this, early sound-board recordings were often affectionately referred to throughout the community as "Bagbies."

Locally, these tapes definitely had an immediate effect, which was clearly demonstrated by the ever-growing audiences at Trax and Flood Zone. Shannon Kearns remembers constantly hearing DMB tapes playing throughout the halls of her on-campus housing residence in Richmond.

"DMB was everywhere. I can't tell you how many times I heard 'Satellite' playing. It started in the undergrad scene and then trickled its way to post-grad and the law school."

With the momentum of early tapers and the cooperation of management through their willingness to allow for recording, a grassroots system was now in place to enable DMB's music to spread beyond Charlottesville and Richmond. UVA and University of Richmond students spread the word to friends on other campuses, sometimes underscoring their positive views about the band with taped show recordings. Friends of friends would come visit UVA, take in a Trax or Flood Zone show, and go back to their own campuses, spreading the word about DMB further.

And with its music trickling out of Charlottesville and Richmond to other locations, it was now time for the band to follow . . .

CHAPTER 3

THE LITTLE RED VAN

DRIVE IN, DRIVE OUT, I'M LEAVING

As DMB's members grew more confident in their collaborative abilities and more attached to the idea of forging a musical future together, they began to expand their reach beyond Charlottesville and Richmond. By late 1992 and with gathering momentum throughout 1993, the band's regular dates at Trax, Flood Zone, and other bars and clubs in the Charlottesville and Richmond areas were supplemented with one-off shows at bars, frat houses, and other campus-affiliated venues, primarily throughout Virginia and the South, but extending northern along the eastern seaboard as 1993 went on. DMB still continued to play Trax and Flood Zone on a weekly basis, but the remaining five days of the week were often spent away from home.

This was a band that was ready to play. And, in a pattern that would prove to be its modus operandi for years to come, when DMB decided to hit the road, it hit it hard. According to DMBAlmanac.com, the band played 148 full-band shows in 1992, 162 in 1993, and 184 in 1994. This would be a relatively punishing schedule for any band, let alone one that was traveling with sparse accommodations. No crowd was too small, no venue too dingy, no fee too low. Although it's nearly impossible to imagine about a band that today can easily sell out major amphitheaters, its early days were often filled with small, dingy, low-paying gigs. But no matter how small the crowd or the venue, the band always came ready to *play*. "They were committed," journalist Andy Garrigue remembers. "They worked hard for it, no question." DMB friend and sometimes-collaborator Tim Reynolds spoke of the toll these intense low-budget touring schedules had on the band, telling *The New York Times* in a May 1998 article, "They would play anywhere, for nothing. They'd look like the living dead when they finished a tour."

DMB piled all of its equipment and small crew into a little red van and set about first the Virginia area and then various spots around the eastern seaboard, concentrating mainly on college towns. The UVA crowd had proven to be an interested and dedicated audience, and it made sense to continue appealing to the college market. Although many of DMB's early frequent stops may seem rather random on paper (Colorado, Georgia, and the Carolinas), the unifying factor among so many of these early gigs was that they offered access to a high percentage of college students. The students would come to shows (often free when they were at frat houses or local bars), become enraptured with the band, and turn their friends on to them as well. Soon word began to spread across other campuses in much the same way it had in Charlottesville and Richmond. Again, this was often accompanied by the distribution of tapes and, from there, perhaps some degree of airplay for the band on college radio stations.

Outside college-focused venues, DMB drew fans by opening for bigger acts of the time such as the Samples, Widespread Panic, and Col.

Bruce Hampton & the Aquarium Rescue Unit at small to midsize clubs. One longtime fan, Nate Vandemark, remembers watching fans emerge before his eyes during DMB's first shows in northeast bars and clubs where they opened for Col. Bruce Hampton & the Aquarium Rescue Unit. "It was small. Imagine going to see a local band at a local club. That's what the scene was. At first no one would really care because they didn't know who DMB was, but after the first few songs everyone was kind of mesmerized, like, 'Wow, these guys really got something going on.'"

Those who witnessed such performances say that the explosive onstage energy DMB is known for today was present even at the earliest of shows, no matter how small the venue. Bruce Hampton, a seasoned musician and then the lead singer of the band Col. Bruce Hampton & the Aquarium Rescue Unit, was witness to some of DMB's earliest shows on the road. In 1992 and 1993, DMB served as an opening act for a handful of shows for Hampton and his band at bar and club gigs in the South and Northeast. Hampton remembers the impressive collective personality of DMB, even in those earliest of days. Of his first show with DMB as an opener, Hampton says, "I remember Dave's enthusiasm—he just seemed overwhelmed like an Olympic runner at the starting gate. Absolutely bubbling over with enthusiasm. I remember thinking, the last time I've seen that was with Otis Redding, who was just about to tear down the walls. Just that enthusiasm and nothing but positive energy."

Although the crowds Hampton saw DMB play for were extremely small, he remembers that the band was able to captivate with its music from the very beginning. Hampton specifically recalls being taken aback by the audience at the first show DMB opened for him at Ziggy's Tavern in Winston-Salem, North Carolina, saying, "There were seven ladies in the front row singing every tune DMB did. And I thought to myself, God, I've never seen an opening band like this. Even though there were only seven people, they were religiously enthralled by it." This fan dedication continued to be a feature of the shows DMB opened up for Hampton and his band. "I remember we did a Monday night in Syracuse or Albany, New York, and, once again, DMB got up to thirty or forty people—all women, singing these songs right along with Dave. And again I thought, God, that's incredible. When women sing your songs on Monday night in a foreign land, it's a good thing. I knew DMB was on its way."

Steven Boyette agrees that the small size of the crowds was compensated for by the enthusiasm both on the floor and on the stage. He remembers one of his first DMB shows at Lewis's in Norfolk, Virginia, on December 28, 1992. "It was absolutely unbelievable. Lewis's is a tiny bar. There couldn't have been more than seventy-five people there, but it was a very engaged crowd. No stage, it was just a back-of-the-bar show. We were standing there at eye level with the band. It was a rip-roaring show; two sets, which was the norm back then. Just fantastic. To this day, it's probably my favorite show. The musicianship was just unbelievable, even in those early days. By this point, it was already fully formed and magical."

Mark Lynn remembers that those early days, when things were less organized than they are today, also lent to some memorable concertgoing experiences of the variety a modern-day DMB fan will likely never witness. "On New Year's Eve 1992, they sold out a black-tie show at the Omni in Richmond. During the show Dave broke a string on his guitar—but he didn't have any extra strings. They had to go borrow some guitar strings from this band called Big City that was playing two blocks down the street. There was this giant break in the show because of that."

Most memorable of all for fans, though, was the intensity that shot off the stage. Vandemark remembers the emotional impact of watching DMB play their first show in Hartford, Connecticut, at Trinity College on November 13, 1993. "I just remember the feeling. They brought the room from so amped up to such a somber mood, right back up to energetic. They started to play 'Blue Water,' and it went from thirty-five minutes of dancing to *boom!* Everyone was just sitting there. I will never forget watching Boyd play what seemed to be such a somber, depressing song that was a completely different vibe than anything else they were playing. And then, as soon as they were done with 'Blue Water'—*bam!* They got the whole crowd dancing again. It was like a roller coaster—they took us up a big hill, then shot us down at full speed."

Clearly, the emotional connection DMB was establishing with crowds paid off. Hampton watched in awe as DMB began to grow exponentially before his very eyes. "After our shows, they went south. Within two months, they were doing fifteen hundred people per night in the South. We would go hang out with them and watch them play, and we were just in shock at the popularity and at how fast it happened. It was, like, a thousand people at Auburn University and fifteen hundred in Atlanta during the workweek. Back then that was unheard of. *Unheard of.*"

To Hampton, it was clear that DMB had a bright future ahead of them, although, admittedly, his scope of success was limited to the environment in which DMB and their brethren bands were playing at the time. "Nobody was playing to much of an audience at all in the early 1990s," Hampton explains of the musical landscape. "DMB was one of the first bands—and Phish and Widespread Panic and Béla Fleck and ourselves. No one was drawing more than three hundred people at the time." But Hampton believed that DMB had the musical prowess and dedication to blast through those numbers. Hampton laughs. "I thought one day they'd probably get three or four thousand people. I had no idea they'd take off like they did, but I knew they had a career in front of them."

To this day, Hampton cannot adequately underscore the degree to which he believes the band's positive energy and enthusiasm launched it along the road to success. "There was just no blockage—absolutely no emotional blockage at all. I mean, you see most bands and you're going to get some grumpy cats and egomaniacs. But everyone in DMB was just so focused. They had a mission, and their path was two hundred yards wide. It was really amazing to see that. *Especially* from a band that was on the road. They were happy, and you don't see shiny, happy people on the road." Most impressive to Hampton was the authenticity of the band's excitement and positivity. "I go back to Dave and just how there was no b.s. to his positivity. There was no cheesiness. It was just like this guy was put here to do this now and he meant business. That's what I loved about him. And all the other guys—very nice cats in the band, all of them."

But the road and heavy touring schedule was not for all of them. After skipping several shows, on March 23, 1993, keyboardist Peter Griesar played his final show with DMB at Trax. Though most fans never knew DMB with Griesar as a member, Steven Boyette remembers, "He added value. The harmonica solo into 'So Much to Say,' the slow keys were beautiful in 'Cry Freedom'—he was good. He was really, really talented."

Aside from serving as Peter's last show, this March 23 gig, which later came to be known as Big League Chew because the gum sponsored the evening, has gone down in DMB history based on the humorous set list soundman Jeff "Bagby" Thomas wrote for it. Included were whimsical titles in lieu of songs' actual names, such as: "Let's Get a Beer" ["I'll Back You Up"]; "The Jumping Song" ["Two Step"]; "Creaming from the Minarets" ["Minarets"]; and "Snoitcelfer Eurt" ["True Reflections"]. One of those names stuck for good in the form of "Heathcliff's Haiku Warriors," a song that debuted that evening and maintained Thomas's moniker for the duration of its short-lived existence.

In attendance at the Flood Zone the evening after Griesar's departure, Boyette remembers, "When we got to the show, Peter wasn't there. During the show, Dave made some sort of reference to Peter not being there, and he just never showed up again. He was there one week, gone the next. For the first week or two, there was a discernable difference. But after that, no."

Though DMB had already built a small following by themselves, in the summer of 1993, they had the opportunity to gain even more widespread exposure through the H.O.R.D.E. (Horizons of Rock Developing Everywhere) festival, which had launched its inaugural tour the year before. In an effort to bring their music to wider audiences, Blues Traveler front man John Popper brought his band, as well as acts like Phish, the Samples, Widespread Panic, Col. Hampton & the Aquarium Rescue Unit, and the Spin Doctors together for a series of summer festivals. Hampton remembers, "There was so much good music and so much quality. Actually, the musicians ran it the first two years as a governed body. We said, 'Let's not charge any more than ten bucks,' which was unbelievable: Aquarium Rescue Unit, Phish, Blues Traveler, DMB, and Widespread Panic for ten bucks. Up north I think we would do about thirty-five hundred in Maine and seven thousand in Jersey. Ten thousand in Atlanta—that was the biggest." By combining their fan bases, H.O.R.D.E. artists were able not only to play bigger venues but also to raise the visibility of several East Coast bands that were struggling to gain a foothold in the mainstream music scene. By introducing larger audiences to a lineup of new, improvisational bands, the H.O.R.D.E. festival created a "scene" of sorts and marked a resurgence of the jam band genre. In July 2000, H.O.R.D.E. cofounder John Popper told *Gig* magazine, "a lot of people got to interact with each other, some great music was made, a great vibe, and we all had a ball. That was completely accidental, and the best thing about it."

From a fan standpoint, Mark Lynn remembers being very excited when DMB signed on to its first H.O.R.D.E. shows in Raleigh and Charlotte, North Carolina, in 1993. "It was the first time they were playing an amphitheater, and it was a really big deal. When DMB got added to the two shows in North Carolina, I thought, Oh, it'd be really great to go see them play a big venue. Which is ironic, looking back."

Even in the midst of all this touring, DMB's hometown shows

continued. By 1993, Nate Vandemark remembers, Trax was completely packed, with would-be attendees being turned away. A Hartford native who made the nine-hour drive just to see DMB play their hometown venue, Vandemark says the whole scene was quite a sight to behold. It was also clear, according to him, that the Charlottesville fan base was extremely well established by that early date.

"I would definitely say the people there were the seeds of the fan base we know today. In 1993, the band was not a nationally known commodity, yet these people at Trax had seen them however many times just because they played there every week. I'll never forget 'Ants Marching' at Trax. It was so energetic—everyone was dancing and having such a great time."

Although this may all be very familiar to today's fans, there were also some elements of Trax shows that sound a little odd from a modern-day DMB perspective. "I remember there was a mosh pit," Vandemark says with a laugh. "I think they were moshing to 'Minarets' or something. It wasn't a huge mosh pit, but it was definitely there up at the front. Back in 1993 I was listening to everything from DMB to Pantera, so mosh pits were nothing new to me at the time. But looking back and thinking about one at a DMB show is kinda weird. I wasn't a big kid when I was in high school, so I remember thinking, I don't want to be in the middle of that. Mosh pits freaked me out."

As DMB began playing for larger and larger crowds in more and more places, the community that had begun to take seed in Charlottesville and Richmond spread further and further. It turned out that in addition to providing a ripe feeding ground for consistent audiences and word of mouth, college campuses provided something else that would prove to greatly benefit DMB and build its community: e-mail access. It may sound strange today, but in the early 1990s, Internet and e-mail access were the exception rather than the rule. College students were one of the earliest cohesive groups to have access to and utilize e-mail, and they put their newfound cyberskills to great use on behalf of DMB.

In October 1993 Minarets Digest (named after the DMB song "Minarets"), the earliest hub of the DMB online community, took root, making information somewhat more obtainable. By today's standards, the mailing list was virtually archaic, with a simple text-only format. But at the time, being part of an online community of any variety was quite a novelty and also fairly cutting edge. As a testament to the innovative nature of online fan conglomerations at the time, Jake Vigliotti (who would, ironically go on to start the massive online DMB hub antsmarching.org a few years later) remembers, "I didn't even have a computer until 1995. I didn't think it was going to take off. I thought the whole computer thing was a fad." Started by a team of college students from UVA, University of Vermont, and Union College in Schenectady, New York, Minarets Digest brought a small but dedicated base of DMB fans together despite their remote locations. This group was heavily slanted toward college students and consisted almost entirely of those matriculating at colleges on the eastern seaboard.

From a modern-day perspective, it's somewhat difficult to imagine how much this online presence changed things—but it did. Prior to fan sites, outside DMB's regular Trax and Flood Zone shows, it was difficult to find out where the band was playing. Mark Lynn laughs, remembering how mystified he was by DMB due to the lack of readily available information at the time. "Really my thought was, what are these guys doing Thursday through Monday when they're not playing Trax or Flood Zone? Are they working regular jobs? I didn't really realize that they were playing all over the place, going to hit the college markets in the Northeast and South and then coming back home for their Tuesday- and Wednesday-night sets. It explains why I used to think, Oh, my God, I swear they're better than they were last week."

In the absence of an official band website or any truly organized way of disseminating information (at that time tour dates were mailed out on postcards), Minarets Digest served the crucial function of keeping fans informed, which was much, much easier said than done in those days—particularly for those outside the Charlottesville and Richmond areas. Today, with set lists available in real time from any number of sources and various e-mail lists, websites, and social networking sites disseminating information en masse, it's nearly impossible to imagine how much digging was required to obtain information prior to Minarets Digest. Finally, there was a simple way to find out about tour dates, read show reviews, check out set lists, and, perhaps most important, set up tape trades. Very quickly DMB's management company, Red Light Management, caught on to Minarets Digest and started disseminating select information to the fan base directly.

Andy Garrigue believes the combination of the emerging Internet, taping, and DMB's dogged touring schedule created the perfect storm. "I remember various members of DMB telling me in an interview that the process was incredible because they'd go to these cities they didn't know on a weeknight and find five hundred people waiting there. Then they'd find a website that was devoted to them. I think part of that is because Coran was a big fan of the Grateful Dead and he knew the value of letting people tape and share the music. That just kind of coincided with websites and e-mail and all those ways of communicating. The technological aspect of it all was just really good timing for the band, I think, in terms of word getting spread."

Aside from providing information about the band and serving as a tape-trading hub, Minarets Digest also allowed fans to stay in touch. At least within this group, communication was no longer limited to shows; fans could now touch base on a consistent basis, no matter where they were. Remote relationships that were built on a shared interest in the band began to emerge—whether they were based on trading or discussing shows or off topic altogether.

As the months went by, the DMB community began to take on a collective personality of its own that has, in large part, continued to remain true to form throughout the years. From the beginning, DMB fans were deeply invested in the music—and quite opinionated. There has always been a certain sense of ownership among the more rabid DMB fans. They know the band's song library inside and out and are adamant about their opinions. "It's quite amazing to read through old Minarets mailing lists," muses antsmarching.org cofounder Jake Vigliotti. "You can take a Minarets post and basically remove the song and replace it with a song today, and it's totally the same thing. They were, like, 'I can't believe they played "Tripping Billies" again. I'm so sick of that.' Now it's the same thing but 'I can't believe they played "Cornbread." I'm so sick of that.'"

In addition to acting as a cybercommunity hub and making it easier to follow DMB, these new band-focused websites vastly expanded the reach of tapes and allowed for a uniform system of taping and trading to be established and disseminated. Before mailing lists and websites came on the scene, making tape trades often involved either careful and extended research or solid relationships within the then-small community. In the absence of sophisticated websites and databases, early trades were made primarily on college campuses or in person at shows.

Jake Vigliotti remembers, "Early on, the only way you really traded was if you were on a college campus and had a friend that liked Dave Matthews too. You'd just call him up and say, 'Hey, I've got this show,' and see if you could exchange tapes." Of course, some tapes did filter into other arenas as well. Mark Lynn remembers taking about fifteen cassettes of a DMB show he'd taped out to West Coast Grateful Dead shows to spread the word in the early nineties. "At that point, I was really trying to reconcile for myself how this little local band that played down the street from my house could be making better music than the Grateful Dead was at that time. I wanted other people to hear DMB too, although I don't know how well received it was in the Grateful Dead circles. They were kind of doing their own thing."

Bill Lakenan explains the impact Minarets Digest had on trading: "At that point it was somewhat of a novelty to be in an online community. Most of the people that were participants were college students through the mid-Atlantic and Northeast. It wasn't a huge group of people, and you got to know who the regular posters were. It was really the only way to get in touch with people for analog tape trading at the time because there was no way to transfer music over the Web and people weren't really burning actual CDs yet."

With the approval of DMB management to tape the shows but no firm taping and trading policy in place, DMB fans began policing themselves by following the lead of taping and trading policies already in effect in Phish and Grateful Dead circles. One longtime trader, Andy Svenson, remembers the old tape-trading rules as dictated and disseminated by early DMB online gathering destinations such as Minarets Digest. "It wasn't the band making the rules, it was the fans. It's what trading had evolved to by this point, with the biggest drivers behind it being the Grateful Dead and Phish. There were generally accepted rules."

The community-dictated rules were fairly straightforward but very strictly enforced: no exchange of money was permitted, only Maxell XL II ninety-minute cassettes could be used to preserve the integrity of the recordings as they moved down through the generations, and dubbed versions had to be copied in real time (as opposed to high-speed dubbing). Dolby noise reduction was also not permitted.

Trading also involved a little bit of strategy. After all, you were more likely to pull off a successful trade if others were interested in the shows you had up for offer. Traders bore this in mind, keeping a careful eye out for special shows that were likely to generate interest at some point down the line. Svenson explains his strategy: "I remember at the beginning just e-mailing everyone to try to get shows—especially shows that looked like they might be desirable for other people. Since you relied on others to mail you the shows you wanted to add to your own collection, you really wanted shows that other people would want."

The trading side of music sharing also served as one of many motivating factors for tapers in these early days, when recordings were more difficult to acquire. Bill Lakenan says, "Taping was sort of a mutually beneficial thing to do because, obviously, the tapes that were most sought after were the ones that were new and nobody had yet. As a taper, you could create those things. So if I really wanted to get sought-after shows on tape, the easiest way to do that was to tape myself. It allowed me to persuade someone to trade that I might not have been able to otherwise."

Once a trade was orchestrated, it would generally work in one of two ways. First, through a tape tree, which had the original DAT (digital audio recording) tape—or the closest thing to it—at the "root" of the tree. People were then assigned to one of an ascending level of "branches." Each branch would copy and send the tape to the next branch and so on. In the days of actual cassettes, this meant that the closer to the "root" of the tree you were, the better-quality recording you would receive, since tapes lost quality with each copy. The most popular and most recent shows were often distributed in the tape-tree format. If a show had been recorded the previous month, for example, a tape tree was the best way to begin disseminating it to the community and circulating it through the trading pool en masse.

The second method of trading was B&P (blank and post). With a B&P trade, fans would identify someone who had a recording they wanted and who was willing to duplicate and mail the show. The recipient would send a blank cassette and return postage to the person in possession of the show, who would make a copy of the cassette and send it back to the requestor via snail mail. This second style of trading might also work as a straight trade, in cases where each party was in possession of a show the other wanted and a swap was initiated.

In the days of B&P, trading was a slow process. First it was necessary to allow the still existent (but today irrelevant) two-week waiting period, which mandates that all tapers be given at least fourteen days postshow to finish their tapes before anyone could so much as begin to request their distribution, to go into effect. After the two weeks passed, the process of finding someone who had a copy of a show or obtaining a spot on a trade tree began. Svenson remembers the arduous waiting process of trading way back when. "Realistically, if you could get a show a month after it occurred, you were doing pretty good. A lot of times it would take a lot longer than that—especially if it was a desirable show. At that point, tapers weren't converting everything over as quickly as they do now. Today, recordings are done in large part straight to computers. Back then DAT tapes were the big thing—and minidisc recorders too, sometimes."

With the somewhat grueling nature of those trades in mind, it was essential to establish a good reputation for yourself in trading circles. Most people realized that if they failed to complete a trade or broke any of the community rules, their chances of getting more shows in the future would diminish. Word traveled throughout the community and "bad trader" lists began to spring up, alerting fans of individuals who should be avoided. Andy Svenson remembers, "It was very well organized, and it almost made it a bit intimidating to get started in trading because you didn't want to mess it up. There were generally accepted rules, and if you broke those rules, you'd end up on a running 'bad trader' list. Bad traders did everything from ripping people off to sending cheap tapes that weren't Maxell XL IIs to dubbing on a boom box or cheap stereo that didn't necessarily have the best tape-copying abilities."

Two of the personality traits most dedicated tapers and traders immediately cite are a tendency toward collecting things and a somewhat obsessive nature. And though the trading rules may seem to reflect the obsessive side of things, they actually had much more to do with creating collections that would stand the test of time. With this in mind, particularly in the days of cassettes, trading guidelines were in place for good reason. Bill Lakenan explains, "I think most tapers have large live collections and fully appreciate the archival responsibility they indirectly shoulder. Not only was it important for everyone to do the right thing and not get this privilege revoked, but everyone was really focused on keeping everything that was circulating of the highest quality. It was self-policed. If a newbie shows up and is doing something horrible in the way they're replicating and trading tapes, people would go out of their way to say, 'Hey, you don't want to do it that way because you're going to pollute the water for all of us.'"

Lakenan's views were shared throughout taping and trading circles. It was considered critical not only to get as many shows out for distribution as possible but also to ensure that the recordings were kept clean and well preserved as they filtered their way through the community. In the early days of trading, when cassettes were the primary recording medium, it was easy to lose quality with each generation. Svenson explains, "One of the things a lot of people don't realize today is that back in the day, tape generation was a big deal. Basically, as you make copies of copies of copies, the quality gets worse and worse. So back in tape-trading days, you always wanted second- or third-generation tapes. A lot of times, if you got below fifth generation, the quality wasn't very good."

In addition to the time-intensive process the more archaic recording processes required, there were other pitfalls. Andy Svenson remembers a long and winding search for a recording of a Vancouver, British Columbia, show. He finally tracked down a taper who had recorded the show, only to find it hadn't ever been released because it was only a partial recording. Svenson laughs. "He wasn't able to tape the whole show because his battery caught on fire!"

Although this wasn't necessarily a frequent occurrence in the 1990s, lesser technology did lend itself to some "interesting" taping rigs. Svenson explains, "Especially in the nineties, there were some creative ways people would try to come up with battery packs that would last for an entire show. Also, the DATs and minidiscs only recorded so long. Whoever was recording the show had to change tapes or change the minidisc at some point. They had to keep a pretty close eye on their battery life and on where their tapes were. Especially with DMB, they had to be conservative when they swapped things out because if the band went into a ten-minute jam, you didn't want to have to cut into the middle of it." Lakenan confirms that early recording systems were prehistoric compared to the gear tapers sport today. "It was a fairly rudimentary taping setup. Just a backpack with a DAT deck and a small set of microphones." Rudimentary taping equipment aside, Svenson points out that the early tapes that emerged from Virginia and other frequent DMB stops in the Southeast tended to be of better quality than those from other locations, for the simple reason that local tapers had the opportunity to perfect their art. "One of the reasons there's such a disparity in the quality of older tapes is because people weren't used to taping in parts of the country where DMB didn't have a huge base."

Because so much time and interaction were required to set up tape trades, perhaps even more important than the actual trades was the fact that they fostered real one-on-one relationships within the DMB community. In many cases, people who completed trades together would eventually meet up at shows and go on to build in-person relationships on the basis of their online trading communication. Before long, fans were compelled to go to DMB shows not only to see the performance but also to hang out with new friends, making the pull of the band's live shows twice as strong. Jake Vigliotti believes the role that trading played in forming the foundation of the DMB community cannot be overstated. "I think the community was really an offshoot of tape trading, which was an offshoot of communication between fans. The way fans communicated with one another was sort of through trading. The thing that kept Minarets going was people going to shows, taping, and telling everyone else, 'Hey, I have the show. Come make a trade.'" From a very early day, then, DMB was about much more than just music for its fans. Although music was certainly the centerpiece, the passion spiraled out into a network of communication and music sharing that has become as integral to the DMB community today as the band itself.

In addition to solidifying a community and keeping DMB's music at the top of fans' minds, the tapes also served a far greater purpose: grass-roots marketing of the most organic and viral kind. Although the band's early scope of traveling was somewhat limited, the tapes took wings. The end result was tapes that spread far beyond DMB's early touring region, which tended not to extend outside of the eastern seaboard and, through 1993, was heavily slanted toward mid-Atlantic and southeastern colleges and clubs. As one taper, John Kelly, points out, "When you're playing a bar in Virginia, you can't really reach Oklahoma." With the help of the tapes, however, the band managed to do exactly that. Kelly continues, "Your friend who saw DMB play when he was visiting Charlottesville can get a tape and play it for his friends. It was like viral marketing—but before the Internet took off." Those tapes tended to spread primarily in college circles and also made their way into other communities that were already spreading tapes of bands such as the Grateful Dead, Phish, and Widespread Panic. Of the effect the tapes had, Boyd explained to *Rolling Stone* in 1996, "People in Colorado knew about us [before DMB toured there]. We'd never been to Alabama before. We'd go to this place, and cars would be lined up down the road, and there'd be all these people going to this big club. We'd be sitting in our red van saying, 'Oh, my God!'"

Ultimately, the tapes had a seeding effect, allowing DMB's music to fly off to places far from home and reach people the band had not yet had the chance to play for. Nate Vandemark considers himself a product of taping and trading. A high school student living in Hartford, Connecticut, in 1993, Nate lived more than five hundred miles away from Charlottesville. With a complete lack of radio play and no shows in the Northeast, it's no surprise that Vandemark had never even heard of the small band in summer 1993. It wasn't until a friend, an avid Grateful Dead tape trader, somewhat inadvertently received a DMB recording in exchange for Grateful Dead tapes that Vandemark accidentally happened upon DMB. "My friend popped the tape in one day while we were hanging out. I couldn't get enough of it. It was all over for me after that."

"It sounded pretty strange at the time," Vandemark remembers. "A lot of people didn't dig the idea of a fiddle player in a rock band; a lot of people didn't dig the idea of no electric guitar, just acoustic. I think that's what I liked about them so much, that it *was* so different. I felt like it was my own personal little secret." The strange sound reeled Vandemark in, and when DMB first ventured northeast to play small-capacity clubs and bars a few months later, Nate was already well aware of their existence and made it his mission to be at those shows. "I started to go see them everywhere they would play in Massachusetts, Connecticut, and New York. I would go see them *everywhere* I heard they were playing."

Others like Nathan started popping up across America, thanks to the tapes. By the time DMB's little red van made its way to new states and venues, it was not uncommon for a preexisting fan base (albeit sometimes a small one), to be waiting with bated breath, ready to sing along with a band they had never before seen played live. Lakenan remembers a conversation he had with DMB violinist Boyd Tinsley in 1997, when Boyd relayed a story about DMB's first show in Atlanta, where the entire crowd was singing DMB's songs, despite a complete lack of airplay—or even a released record. "Boyd attributed that to tapers," Lakenan says. Early tapers took great pride in doing what they saw as their part in spreading the music of this tiny band, helping to take the music far beyond its home.

Thanks to the tapes and the band's heavy touring schedule, by the time DMB released its first album, *Remember Two Things*, on their independent label Bama Rags on November 9, 1993, it had already created a buzz for itself in certain circles. *Remember Two Things* consisted of a combination of live and studio-recorded songs, all of which had already been played at live shows. Despite the fact that the album didn't contain any as-yet-unheard material, this was the first time fans had the opportunity to have official recordings in hand. Although DMB had already been approached by record labels, it made a conscious decision to release its debut album independently, under its own terms. In a February 1, 1995, interview with the *Bangor Daily News,* Matthews stated, "It's been a consistent climb, rather than a series of leaps and plateaus. We kind of orchestrated things that way, to build it and make it more real. If it had blown up really fast, it could have overwhelmed us."

By the time the album's release rolled around, DMB already had a steady enough following that the Charlottesville and Richmond indie music store Plan 9 Music felt local demand warranted a special midnight release. Andy Garrigue, then an employee at Plan 9, remembers working that night. "People lined up, and we ran it like when tickets go on sale for a hot concert. We gave people numbers, so there was no line jumping, and it was all very civilized. Everyone was just really psyched and in a good mood— people were very excited. As I recall, between the two stores we sold twelve hundred copies that first night. We were flabbergasted by that amount." For fans of the time, Garrigue explains, the release was a big deal. "Because DMB had built up such a hometown crowd and had such a big following in Richmond, I think we just got a sense people were really excited about this release. And *Remember Two Things* continued to sell steadily and very well for a long time. We were continually restocking that thing." Plan

9 wasn't the only location moving the independently distributed album. In a February 1994 article for *Style Weekly,* Garrigue wrote, "According to Bigshots Records out of Athens, Georgia, who shipped 12,500 DMB discs in the first two weeks, 'first-day sales of this album were bigger than any artist outside REM and Widespread Panic.'" Over the course of the next two years, *Remember Two Things* would go on to sell more than 100,000 copies, largely through Red Light Management direct mail orders and at-show sales. (In addition to these early sales as an independent record, *Remember Two Things* was rereleased by RCA on June 24, 1997, and officially certified platinum in July 2002.)

Even though he had witnessed large crowds on a firsthand basis at the Flood Zone and expected DMB would continue to grow, Steven Boyette remembers being shocked at the crowd he found waiting outside Plan 9 on the album's release night. "I can definitely point to the *Remember Two Things* record release as the moment when I realized things were getting big. I bought my CD at midnight, and there was a very long line. Seeing the line the way it was that night, I knew it was important to see DMB while I still could because it wasn't going to be this way forever. It was shocking, getting there at 11:30 P.M. to see a huge group of people just like me already waiting. There was definitely a part of me that was like, 'Wait a minute. This is my secret thing. What's everyone doing here?'"

Mark Lynn also remembers the release of *Remember Two Things* as a marker moment and the point where he realized DMB was spreading rapidly. "I was in Athens, Georgia, at the time it came out, and I remember going into Wuxtry Records and seeing *Remember Two Things* there. I was blown away by the fact that their CD was in Georgia. It was an awesome feeling." It wasn't always that easy to get your hands on a copy of the disc, though. One fan, Christopher Smith, remembers, "I first heard DMB in the spring of 1994, on a college radio show in Texas. The student DJ, a Virginia transplant, played a cassette he'd gotten from a friend at the UVA.

He played 'Ants Marching,' and I was immediately hooked. I tried to find an album in my local music store, but the workers there had never even heard of the band. When I told one of the employees I had heard them on a college radio show, he suggested I try the independent record store on the other side of town. A few days later, I had my very own copy of *Remember Two Things* on CD. I still have it to this day."

Remember Two Things marked a turning point for DMB. In many ways, it stands alone in terms of DMB's recorded library, because it *is* so small and independent, in stark contrast to the albums that would follow in years to come. While most of the tracks were live recordings from shows, in a March 1994 article with *Hampden-Sydney,* Dave explains the "homemade" nature of the little studio work that was required for the album, saying of the thunderstorm and cricket-chirping sounds that mark the close of the *Remember Two Things* CD, "There was a huge thunderstorm outside where we were recording. So we just took a blank out there and recorded it. We did the same thing with the crickets."

On the heels of the *Remember Two Things* release, the band signed its first record deal with RCA, inking the contract just five hours after that midnight release. For DMB and its manager, Coran Capshaw, the decision to sign with a major record label *after* its first official release was an exercise in pragmatism. Matthews told *The Advocate* of Baton Rouge on February 17, 1995, "As my manager always says, if RCA fell off the planet right now, we'd be fine. . . . A strong enough business gives us a position of power as far as being able to bargain [with RCA]. We're not afraid of them saying 'OK, we're not going to work with you anymore.' We're able to say no to the record company."

Ultimately, DMB's deal with RCA is one of the biggest testaments to the power of tape trading. With all of the tapes flitting around from one person to the next in the early 1990s, one of them landed in the hands of RCA A&R (Artist and Repertoire) executive Bruce Flohr, who obtained it through John Brodey, an intern from Colgate University. It was that tape that initially turned Flohr on to DMB. Flohr's colleague Pete Robinson had also recently become aware of DMB's existence, and the two teamed up to bring the band to RCA. Confident that DMB had a strong future based on the credit of its live act and the fan base it had already managed to create on their own, the RCA deal was signed, sealed, and delivered.

Andy Garrigue, who interviewed Dave and Coran at the Flood Zone release party on November 10, 1993, remembers the excitement in the air. "They signed the deal with RCA at five A.M. that morning after they witnessed the midnight sale and the numbers were coming in. It was a beautiful time to chart their future. That was the first night I met Dave. He was very humble and appreciative of what was happening; just going with the flow."

Capshaw, for his part, was already thinking ahead. Garrigue remembers, "He said he was a huge fan of the Grateful Dead and Jerry Garcia Band, and when he saw DMB—and particularly Dave—he saw every potential for them to be as big as the Dead. I thought, Wow, that's a pretty long-reaching vision for a band that's just released their first indie release. Coran had the long view. He thought DMB would have an arc that could go for twenty to twenty-five years and maintain an extremely loyal fan base. His vision was impressive to me, but back then, of course, I didn't know it would all come to pass." As he interviewed Capshaw and Matthews upstairs at the Flood Zone, Garrigue had a perfect view of fans waiting for the release show to begin. "I could see the crowd snaking down in the line below. They were all hyped up. People knew they had the golden ticket for that show."

Even with an album on the shelves to supplement the already circulating tapes, the DMB community continued to do its part to spread the music. A Red Light Management posting on Minarets on October 15, 1993, stated, "Since this disc is not being distributed through any of the major distributors, we need to build a buzz through consumer demand . . . so ask the store." Fans took the task seriously, with a poster writing the following day, "I urge all of you out there to get your local record companies to get this disk [sic]. They probably aren't going to get it otherwise, especially if you live north of the Mason-Dixon line. So keep bugging your record store and play the album for all your friends so they will go to buy the album."

Things were now happening quickly. In addition to signing the RCA deal, on November 22, 1993, DMB charted for the first time, with *Remember Two Things* listing as the top independent release on the *College Music Journal* chart. While it was certainly exciting for DMB's earliest loyal followers to see the band expanding their reach, for some it was also a little bittersweet. One longtime fan, Matt McKibben, remembers experiencing some mixed emotions when he saw DMB play the 620-person capacity Georgia Theatre in Athens, Georgia, a few months later on February 5, 1994. "It was almost like a secret for me because they were so unknown when I got into them—no one else really knew them. I almost felt like I was letting people in on my music at the Georgia Theatre show. I had reservations for a minute when the band got big; it was bittersweet. On one hand I was like, 'Wow, DMB made it. This is great—we're gonna get more!' Because for a while, I wasn't sure we *were* going to get more. But at the same time, I had to hear other people's opinions on the band, and before DMB was just this thing I had for me, that was a part of my own little world. Now it was for everybody."

Nate Vandemark agrees that those early days contained a thrilling element of having caught on to something that didn't yet belong to everyone else. "I kind of felt like it was my little secret when I would go see them in Northampton, Massachusetts, and Hartford. The first time I saw them they weren't even the main act—they were opening for Col. Bruce Hampton & the Aquarium Rescue Unit." Even after the band exploded onto the national scene, though, Vandemark was able to hang on to vestiges of this early sense of discovery. "I've always known from when I first discovered DMB that they were my little secret. And still, to this day, I sort of feel like they are. What the band has meant to me over the last seventeen years is my secret—it's just for me and not for anybody else to understand. And I love that I have that."

Though the Flood Zone shows continued, Steven Boyette says, "I had this conscious realization that I needed to stop and take it all in because it wasn't going to be like this much longer. By that point I was waiting in line to get in and it was packed to the rafters. I knew it was going to end, and eventually it did. It was inevitable they were going to get bigger. Certainly bigger than the Flood Zone." Boyette was right. As DMB became less and less of a secret, its regular hometown shows at Trax and Flood Zone began to trickle out. Mark Lynn remembers, "The shows sort of faded out when DMB got too big for the Flood Zone. They would still do occasional appearances at both venues for a handful of years, but never on a regular basis like it was before." According to Lynn, this transition was a gradual one. "At first it was like, 'Oh, they're not playing this week, but they'll be back next week.' Then it was twice a month, then once a month. I remember having a sense of finality at that last Flood Zone show in September 1994."

As locals were adjusting to the fact that DMB was quickly outgrowing the local home-stand shows that had marked its first few years as a professional act, so too was the band. According to Stefan Lessard, "It's funny because at the time we were playing places like the Fox Theatre in Boulder, Colorado [with a seating capacity of just under 700]. It's one of those things where everyone's like, 'Can you believe you're playing an amphitheater?' and I didn't even know these things existed. For me an amphitheater was, like, in a park. I didn't know this existed."

With the momentum that had now gathered, though, Stefan and his bandmates were about to find out just how big things could get.

THE BIG THREE

I CAN SEE THREE CORNERS FROM THIS CORNER

D MB now entered the next era of its career. Its first three albums with RCA—affectionately referred to as the Big Three by fans—marked what many consider to be the band's creative golden years. Collectively, *Under the Table and Dreaming* (1994), *Crash* (1996), and *Before These Crowded Streets* (1998) contain many of the songs that DMB is not only most famous for (such as "Ants Marching," "Crash into Me," "Satellite," and "Too Much"), but also songs that have gone on to be timeless live anthems of sorts in the many, many years that have followed. For fans, songs such as "Two Step," "#41," "Dancing Nancies," "Warehouse," "Dreaming Tree," and "Pig" are like a good pair of well-worn jeans: they change shape over time but become more comfortable and beloved as each year goes by.

The songs recorded during the Big Three years were in some cases a throwback that tied the band's earlier years to their entrance onto the mainstage of America's musical landscape. As a live act for so long before it hit the recording studio, DMB had a virtual library of songs that had already morphed, shape-shifted, and gained a presence on the fan periphery well before they were committed to studio tracks.

It was with several of these preexisting songs that DMB went to record its first RCA album with the English producer Steve Lillywhite in May 1994. Lillywhite, who had already made a name for himself producing major acts such as Peter Gabriel, U2, and the Rolling Stones, had a good sense of what the powerhouse band could do live and felt he could translate that sensibility into a studio format. When asked whether he was daunted by the prospect of wrangling DMB's unusual sound and jammy tendencies into album format during an August 2008 episode of NPR's *World Cafe,* Lillywhite explained, "Lots of people look at unusual things as problems. I look at unusual things as . . . something I can get my teeth into." With Lillywhite, DMB entered Bearsville Studio, a converted barn just outside Woodstock, New York, to record *Under the Table and Dreaming.* In a nice example of the circular nature that has marked DMB's career, Bearsville Studios was originally opened by Albert Grossman, who had managed DMB friends and Charlottesville music group the Deal prior to his death.

For Dave, it was important that there was a delineation between the live show recordings that already existed in abundance and the band's first major label studio effort. In a March 1994 article he told the *Hampden-Sydney,* "I don't want people to say, 'Hey, I've already got that stuff on my bootleg.' I'd like to put out a record that doesn't sound like us live . . . one that has the power [of the live shows], but has a little more clarity." For this reason, the band was excited about letting up their break-neck touring pace to relax into recording *Under the Table and Dreaming.* In the same interview, Dave explained, "We'll have two months, which is just heaven. The only studio work we've done has been like, 'Okay, we're going to record an album—you have four days.' And it's really hard to get anything going."

For this first major label album, DMB was armed with a stable of songs that had already been solidly road-tested during their intense touring schedule over the course of the band's career, a couple of which had previously been included as live tracks on *Remember Two Things* ("Ants Marching" and "Satellite"). Despite this, Lillywhite's production infused many of DMB's time-tested songs with new vim and vigor. Coupled with the band's tendency to improvise both musically and lyrically when playing live, *Under the Table* offered old fans a somewhat different incarnation of DMB from the one they were accustomed to.

For some fans who had been around for a while, this more "produced" sound was an unwelcome change and represented the end of being on the inside loop of an indie band. For others, it signified the successful culmination of their collective efforts to spread the word about DMB. Welcome or not, though, it certainly marked the end of an era. As one fan wrote in Minarets Digest two days before the album's release, "I'm in a kind of pensive mood today about the Dave Matthews Band. Monday, September 26, 1994 is the last day of an era for the band and all its fans . . . and thus it's also a time for reflection and anticipation."

While older fans were adjusting, new fans were coming onboard. One fan, Tara Hanshaw Lewis, remembers the impact the album had on her. "I got my first DMB album, *Under the Table and Dreaming,* when I was fifteen, and that was it; I was hooked. I spent hours listening to it, locked in my bedroom, escaping into the beauty, joy, and solace of the music. Every album was and still is incredible, and the lyrics have shaped my perception of the world. DMB is the sound track of my life."

In an effort to highlight DMB's distinctly acoustic sound, the band and Lillywhite decided to bring Charlottesville friend and musician Tim Reynolds into the studio. Together, Dave and Tim laid down dual tracks for *Under the Table,* resulting in a full acoustic sound that not only immediately set DMB apart from the vast majority of its musical counterparts of the time but also went a long way toward re-creating DMB's bold live energy in recorded form. Lillywhite appreciated the appeal of DMB as a live act, and, in a further effort to capture this energy on the studio album, many of the tracks were laid down as full-band recordings, as opposed to mixing single cuts of individual instruments together during production.

Although *Under the Table* is acoustically driven, it also served as a thorough introduction of the entire band to new audiences. Throughout the course of the album, each member of DMB is individually featured, with lead violin and horn sections and Carter Beauford and Stefan Lessard's driving rhythms to hold it all together. Lillywhite's production style was polished but playful, a tactic that underscored the pickup, improvisational spirit of the band. A feature of Lillywhite's production (which would remain consistent throughout his tenure with the band) is the incorporation of background noise, such as the boisterous hooting and hollering running in the background of "What Would You Say." Little touches like this added yet another element of "liveness" to the recordings and went a long way toward preserving the vibe DMB created onstage.

In addition to the already stark contrast between their music and that of their peers, in many ways the diversity of the songs included on *Under the Table* made DMB even more difficult to pin down to a preexisting musical category. "What Would You Say" has a bluegrassy feel, highlighted by Blues Traveler front man John Popper's harmonica solo; "Rhyme and Reason" is a driving, angry song with Matthews growling over beating rhythms; in many ways LeRoi's lilting horn serves as the lead just as much as Dave's vocals in "Lover Lay Down"; and the graceful full-instrumental "#34" (hidden as the thirty-fourth track on the original CD) that ended the album was a true anomaly for the rock music market. Of this eclecticism, upon the album's release, *Rolling Stone* critic Paul Evans wrote, "Almost unclassifiable, the Dave Matthews Band sound like four or five groups in one."

Part of the reason the band's sound was so diverse was, of course, the different backgrounds and expertise of the members. The combination of Stefan's youthful funk sensibility, LeRoi's jazzy roots, and Boyd's rocked-out translation of the normally orchestral violin created unique music that melded funk, jazz, rock, folk, and world music to create an entirely new entity. But in addition to the members' varied musical influences, the songs on this first studio album also reflected the experiences and general viewpoints Dave and the band had developed over several years. And as they prepared to go into the studio to make the album that would change their professional lives forever, Dave experienced a tragedy that would also alter his personal life irrevocably.

In January 1994, Dave's sister Anne, who was still living in South Africa, was murdered, leaving behind two children. On tour in Colorado at the time, DMB improvised while Matthews went to South Africa to mourn with his family. On January 15, 1994, the Samples filled in at the scheduled Fox Theatre (Boulder, Colorado) show for DMB, playing with Carter, LeRoi, and Boyd; all proceeds from that show were donated to Anne Matthews's children. The same thing occurred the following night at Fox Theatre as well, and the show was officially dubbed the Anne Matthews Benefit Show, again with the proceeds going to the surviving family members.

This incident profoundly affected Dave, and the repercussions of this tragic death (coupled with the earlier death of his father) can clearly be seen in his lyrics. (*Under the Table and Dreaming* includes a dedication to Anne on the inside cover of the CD.) In a December 1996 article with *Rolling Stone*, Dave explained the collective influence his sister's and father's deaths had on his songwriting. "I think a lot of the reason my choruses include, 'Make the best of it'—or maybe 'Be grateful, anyway'—is because the different tragedies that hit our family were also an *inspiration* for me. They make me want to live now, *desperately*—and to try to affect things positively."

But it's not all carpe diem; songs such as "Pay for What You Get" and "Rhyme and Reason" spoke of common human trials and tribulations such as grief, loss, disillusionment, anger, and coping. Such lyrics resonated deeply with the young and coming-of-age college audience targeted by DMB. As one fan, Josh Angle, puts it, "This music helps me understand situations, whether pain of death, lost love, or just outright having fun." Many fans who found DMB during this period cite an emotional attachment to the lyrics, which reeled them in and bonded them to the band's music for years to come.

Matt McKibben, who received *Under the Table* as a gift from his father for Christmas in 1994, relied heavily on the album in the months that followed his father's death months later in August 1995. McKibben says, "I don't know how connected the two were for me at the time, but the music definitely helped me through a lot of bad times back then. The music was for me, then and now, almost like therapy. [The music] kind of took front seat when it needed to. When negative forces were trying to lead, the band and the music and the lyrics and everything just kind of said 'no' and led me in a more positive direction. I don't know where I'd be today without the music."

Though the themes of death and grief are certainly interwoven into *Under the Table,* so too is their antidote. Those darker tones are underscored with lyrics that speak to the urgency of living: of finding yourself, being yourself, and celebrating life and love. Ultimately, it's a well-rounded album not only musically but thematically as well. The music addresses the kind of questions that plague the youth of every generation. In "Dancing Nancies," for example, Matthews wonders what alternate routes his life could have taken had his situation been different. This somewhat heavy lyrical theme, continued throughout the course of the song, is counteracted by an infectious salsalike rhythm and Boyd's uplifting fiddle strokes, which add a joyful undercurrent to Dave's weighty lyrics. After questioning his place in life throughout the course of "Dancing Nancies," Matthews ultimately determines that perhaps the answer is simply to let go and give in to the music and the moment. For one fan, Chrissy Massone, the draw of songs such as "Dancing Nancies" is Matthews's expression of the thoughts that people rarely speak about. "When I heard 'Dancing Nancies' for the first time, it was like a meeting of the souls with Dave, because when I was a kid I would always look in the mirror and ask, 'Why am I who I am? Why wasn't I someone else?' It was very comforting to know Dave asked himself those questions too. I was going through a rough time in my life and didn't feel quite so alone. The entire *Under the Table* album kept me from going over the deep end."

Therein lies the formula that ultimately drew more than six million people to *Under the Table and Dreaming.* Unexpected musical combinations that often veer toward the celebratory and joyful belie Matthews's darker, more pensive lyrics. In a 2009 interview with CBS's *Sunday Morning*, Matthews said, "I do write about death a lot. I don't like to overuse the whole seize-the-day thing, but I think the fact that we're all gonna die is a pretty good reason to stop complaining." This combination is at the very heart of many of the songs included on *Under the Table* that have gone on to become anthems of sorts for DMB audiences. Susan Bible remembers the powerful effect of the album, her introduction to DMB, had on her. "I was traveling home from work along White Sands Boulevard in Alamogordo, New Mexico, in 1995. I always listened to a great alternative radio station from Las Cruces, a New Mexico State University college town. 'Ants Marching' began, and I was completely mesmerized. What was I hearing here? How can a rock song have horns and violins and the most unusual singing voice I've ever heard with crazy strong drumbeats? *Who the hell is this?* I had to find out immediately, and as soon as I did, I purchased *Under the Table.* It was one of those rare musical experiences: I put the CD in and listened—*really listened*—to every song. And every single song was outstanding . . . meaningful."

Released on September 27, 1994, *Under the Table* debuted at number thirty-four on the *Billboard* Top 200, an auspicious position for an album that contained thirty-four tracks and closed with a song titled "#34." Over the course of the next few months, five singles were released from the album, including "What Would You Say," "Ants Marching," "Satellite," "Jimi Thing," and "Typical Situation." This was bolstered by the release of DMB's first music video for "What Would You Say," a somewhat psychedelic piece that featured a scrawny, shuffling singer leading a group of mismatched-looking characters in a live performance. On March 7, 1995, DMB earned its first gold certification for its RCA debut; two months later, on May 8, *Under the Table* was officially certified platinum (in the years that followed, *Under the Table* continued to sell, eventually going six times platinum). The album topped off at number eleven on *Billboard*, spending a total of 116 weeks on the charts. It also earned DMB its first Grammy nominations, with "What Would You Say" nominated for Best Rock Vocal and Best Music Video (the Grammys were ultimately awarded to Blues Traveler for "Run Around" and Janet and Michael Jackson for "Scream").

Not only did DMB garner a wider audience from the release of *Under the Table,* it also got the attention of music critics. Upon its release, *Rolling Stone* wrote, "South African expatriate Dave Matthews leads a Virginia quintet whose major-label debut is one of the most ambitious releases of '94. With an arsenal that includes reeds and violin backing Matthews' gorgeous vocals, they've got chops to kill. But it's the complex harmonies and subtle rhythmic shifts of songs like 'Satellite' and 'The Best of What's Around' that really slay." Of course, it wasn't all praise. *Entertainment Weekly* graded the album a C+ in its November 11, 1994, issue and went on to say, "Their fancy folk-guitar picking and Latin percussion passages prove these biracial Virginia jam-rockers have chops. But the band mostly offers a formless brand of laid-back eclecticism, tainted by smarmy inner-awareness poetry."

In the midst of recording and releasing *Under the Table*, DMB continued its intense touring schedule, playing just under two hundred shows throughout the course of 1994. While they still continued to hit college towns, that year also saw DMB expand its reach, serving as the opening act for bands such as the Samples, Blues Traveler, and Phish. Though DMB opened a few shows for Big Head Todd and the Monsters at Red Rocks, by just a few months later the bill would flip, with Big Head Todd opening for DMB at several venues. In the later months of 1994, DMB began visiting some markets it had not yet hit, including California, Oregon, and Texas. During the summer, DMB once again joined the H.O.R.D.E. lineup. Matt McKibben, who saw them play the festival in Richmond in both 1993 and 1994, remembers the vast difference twelve months made. "H.O.R.D.E. 1994 was the last time I plugged into the sound board. It just got bigger and bigger after that point. They really came out and tore it up. They did 'Jimi Thing' and rocked the house. Boyd came out with the Allman Brothers. It was just a great day."

The Bagby sound-board recordings that had infiltrated the trading market during the band's earlier years were suddenly becoming more problematic due to the increasingly widespread interest in DMB. Because CD burners were still too expensive to be a common household item, a few entrepreneurial spirits found a rather lucrative market for bootleg shows. Individuals would copy crisp sound-board recordings of live DMB shows and burn them onto CDs for record stores to sell as "imports." Those "import" CDs would then be sold to customers for up to $60 a pop. DMB fought against record stores that sold illegal products and issued a statement that expressed its disapproval in no uncertain terms: "We would like to thank those of you who have been helping us with the bootleg CD problem. For those of you who are unaware of what's been going on we would like to let you know that the Dave Matthews Band has always encouraged the taping of our performances, but only for personal use, including trading, as outlined in the Taping Policy Statement. We feel that each show is unique and want to offer our fans the opportunity to re-create the live experience through the audio reproduction of our shows. Lately, however, the proliferation of bootleg CD recordings of our concerts has become a concern to us. Bootleg CD's [*sic*] are not only excessively priced and of inferior quality, but primarily, they are an illegal use of Dave Matthews Band material and a rip-off of our fans and the band. Due to the efforts of a few unscrupulous tapers the privilege of recording live performances has been jeopardized. Those of you who have passed along information about bootleg CD's [*sic*] have been very instrumental in our fight against these bootleggers."

Although DMB's management had historically been cooperative with taping and trading, the distribution of live recordings for profit was strictly prohibited. Profiting off recordings such as this went completely against the spirit of taping, which was designed to build community and spread free music. For a time, there was some concern among the taping community that bootlegging would bring DMB's taping policy to an end altogether. Bill Lakenan remembers, "There was a lot of concern that 'Crap! A few bad apples are going to ruin this for all of us.' I think everyone was concerned that would foster a very reasonable backlash from Red Light to shut down taping."

In an effort to counteract bootlegging, by early 1995, fans were no longer allowed to plug directly into the DMB sound board. Lakenan recalls word spreading in 1994 that the days of sound-board pulls would be drawing to a close at the Marriott Richmond New Year's Eve show that year. Of that show, Lakenan says, "There were a lot of rumors circulating that it would be the last sound-board seed, so all the tapers were sort of giddy and recognized the significance of that show." Indeed, by early 1995, the days of sound-board pulls had come to an end. "It got out of control," Mark Lynn remembers. "Bagby would let us plug into the sound board. As taping caught on, you'd just see these stacks of cassette players and boom boxes, all plugged into one another to get a board pull." The repercussions of the loss of sound-board privileges had a serious impact on the world as DMB tape traders knew it. With show recording now limited to freestanding mics, the community experienced a significant decrease in recording quality in the years that followed the sound board ban.

The DMB roller coaster moved with increasing speed throughout 1995. Consistent touring throughout a far broader area (including summer dates in Europe), at larger venues, continued tape trading, and ever-increasing media attention and visibility was working its magic. On February 14 and 15 of that year, DMB was given the distinct honor of playing a set of its own songs (including "Granny," "Lover Lay Down," and "Help Myself," among others), backed by the Richmond Symphony Orchestra. Because of its location and the unique setup of the show, many of the fans in attendance that night still remembered DMB as a hometown act. With its increasing popularity and wider-ranging touring schedule, the Trax and Flood Zone shows had become but a memory, so those shows with the Richmond Symphony Orchestra were a special occasion of sorts. In attendance that night, Bill Lakenan remembers, "The show itself was incredibly powerful. The arrangement was very well done. I don't know much about symphonies and orchestras, but I vaguely remember that the guy that arranged it with Dave was a fairly progressive, modern kind of guy and really did some neat things in backing the band with the whole orchestra. I vaguely remember hearing 'Warehouse,' and the crescendos were just overpowering. It really was incredible. I remember walking out of there feeling mostly blown away. Maybe it was more my age at the time, but it felt very orchestral. Everyone was having a good time. There was a little bit of tension in the room because you had some people that wanted to hoot and holler and, during some of the quiet patches, a lot of people would react to that, like, 'This is a fine arts event, pipe down.'"

Just over a week later, DMB played on a much different stage, putting in its first national media television performance on *The Late Show with David Letterman.* Shortly thereafter, the band appeared on the April 15, 1995, episode of *Saturday Night Live.* David McNair remembers this as the moment when he came to the realization that DMB had made it far outside the confines of Trax and Charlottesville. "I remember when they were first on *Saturday Night Live,* going down to Miller's, and David was there. He'd normally just sit down and have a beer. But we sat down to have a beer that night and people just started sort of gravitating around the table and mooching in. I was like, 'What the heck's going on?' It just sort of changed."

According to the journalist Bill Ramsey, this attention was perhaps more surprising to Matthews himself (or, as Ramsey referred to the musician in his "DMBeat" column, "The Dave") than anyone else. "Being a native son, Dave was a local phenomenon—something I felt took him aback. You'd often find him at local coffee shops and clubs or just walking down the mall in Charlottesville. There were rabid fans to be sure, but most people treated him with an air of, 'Oh, hi Dave.' There was a 'Dave fever' building with cover stories in *Rolling Stone,* new albums, and websites . . . leading the way."

Not only did things change for DMB and the way people perceived it, but, according to McNair, the massive success the band ultimately achieved affected Charlottesville as a whole. "It definitely changed downtown," McNair muses. "It really changed the whole town a lot. A good way to explain it is this: look what happened to Miller's. Miller's was just an old dive bar people hung out at—now it's, like, a tourist attraction. That's *weird.*"

Despite everything else going on, DMB's primary attention remained where it always had: on the live shows. Although they were relatively new on the national scene, the members of DMB were, at this point, veterans of the road. In a March 19, 1995, review in the St. Paul *StarTribune,* a reviewer wrote the following about DMB, which, notably, didn't even serve as the main act of the evening but rather opened for Big Head Todd and the Monsters: "Judging by Saturday's sweet and sophisticated performance, Virginia's Dave Matthews Band is following a whole other musical map from its fellow workhorses. In fact, the band looks and sounds ready to join the truly elite ranks of American light rock, bringing to mind the prime work of the Grateful Dead, Stephen Stills and even a little Steely Dan. Some moments even rivaled the beauty and strength of Van Morrison in his mellow, mystical period throughout the 1980s."

May 10, 1995, saw one of DMB's most heralded shows to date, at the unlikely venue Yoshi's, a jazz club and Japanese restaurant in Oakland, California. Recorded as an acoustic radio show performance for San Francisco's KFOG radio station while the band was playing a two-night stand at the nearby Warfield, this show featured the debut of "Don't Burn the Pig" (which would evolve into "Pig" on the album *Before These Crowded Streets*) and what is commonly regarded as one of the band's best renditions of the never-released "#40," a song with somewhat elusive and constantly in-flux lyrics. This particular version of "#40" is so renowned that thirteen years later, at the June 20, 2008, Saratoga Performing Arts Center (SPAC) in Saratoga Springs, New York, Matthews said in reference to the Yoshi's "#40" lyrics, "I can taste it, but I'm real full. So what I may do is try and learn that thing 'cause my memory is not as good as yours. As the years have gone by, I have more and more problems with my word retrieval unit. . . . I'm gonna look for it tonight, and when I find it I'm gonna bring it to school tomorrow." To this day, it is almost assured that most avid DMB fans have a recording of the Yoshi's show in their collection.

While on this same West Coast run, DMB served as the opening act for the Grateful Dead during their May 19–21 stand at the University of Nevada at Las Vegas's 40,000-capacity Sam Boyd Stadium, the largest venue DMB had played to date. Former Deadhead Dr. Barry Barnes (who would go on to become a professor of leadership at Nova Southeastern University, where he has spent years examining the lure of the collective as a Grateful Dead scholar), remembers seeing DMB open up these Nevada shows. "I saw DMB three times in 1995, when they opened for the Dead in Vegas. It was a bitchin' hot day with three really great sets. I remember Dave making an announcement from the stage saying, 'Wow, we're not used to this. This is the same crowd we saw yesterday. We can't play the same show we played yesterday.' It seemed to me like this was an interesting point for DMB. They played three really great shows; it was spectacular."

Though only symbolic (and obviously something of which everyone was completely unaware of at the time), as one of the Grateful Dead's last shows before Jerry Garcia's death just a few months later on August 9, there is retrospectively a nice sort of passing of the guard with these Nevada shows. Upon Garcia's death, DMB found themselves at Berkeley's Greek Theatre (a venue frequented by the Bay Area–based Dead) just two days later and dedicated a rendition of "Eyes of the World" to Jerry. As a final passing of the guard, DMB inherited some of the Dead's touring sound system, which debuted at the Richmond, Virginia, *Crash* release show in 1996 (this show was released as *Live Trax, Vol. 4* in September 2005).

In attendance at the August 11, 1995, Berkeley show, one fan, Brad Adams, remembers the scene. "Jerry died two days prior. The mood in the Bay Area was *really* weird. Everyone was kind of sad and somber and pretty bummed. When Dave made mention of Jerry's passing and then said they were going to play a song they'd never played before, there was this little buzz around like, 'What song's this gonna be? They gotta do something for Jerry.' Once DMB started playing 'Eyes of the World,' a lot of the people in the crowd knew what it was right away. It was probably a ten- or twelve-minute song—it was really cool. When it finished, the crowd kind of gave Jerry an ovation."

Although there are certainly many differences musically between DMB and the Grateful Dead, the similarities between their improvisational live shows, which sweep crowds up and take them along for the ride, cannot be discounted. As Jim DeRogatis wrote in the April 30, 1996, issue of *Rolling Stone*, "Spin Doctors and Dave Matthews Band are among those groups vying to continue the ideals of the live Dead, exploring diverse sounds from a rock perspective in a commitment to free-flowing improvisation." Based on his studies and personal experiences, Dr. Barnes believes it's this musical spirit that creates a collective—the phenomenon that keeps fans coming back to live shows time and time again: "Listening to music on your own—no matter how wonderful and visceral the listening experience is—is certainly not the same thing as being with a group of like minds. That's where the magic really, really happens. Any band that puts itself out on the edge to do something creative rather than re-creating the same show over and over understands this. Bands like the Grateful Dead and DMB are very aware they would not be the same band without this living, breathing entity that's out there when they play. Jung talks about the collective consciousness as well. It's nothing new, but certainly in our world today we don't talk about the things we can't touch, measure, taste, or feel—those things that aren't tangible or concrete. This is certainly one of those things that's not concrete. It's *almost* tangible—it's pretty close to tangible when you're there. To me, it's the perfect representation of synergy, which means that the whole is greater than the sum of its parts. If I give a hundred percent, I'm going to get a hundred ten percent back, which is true magic. We're talking about magic. The audience is in tune with the music, and the band is certainly in tune with the music. And somehow we're all able to link up there."

That night at Berkeley, Brad Adams experienced precisely the sort of magic Dr. Barnes references. A few months prior to the August 11, 1995, show, Adams was turned on to DMB while riding in his friend's car. Before turning on a cassette taper pull titled simply "DMB," this friend told Adams, "Everyone should *experience* DMB's music." Adams remembers that the comment seemed strange to him at the time: "Nobody had ever said anything like that to me about music before. It's usually like, 'Oh, yeah, these guys rock. Check 'em out.' But *experience* the music? That was new." Adams was intrigued, and a few months later, when DMB made one of its first California stops at Berkeley's Greek Theatre, he decided to check them out.

"As the show started, I was just really surprised at how many people had packed that place because I wasn't sure that an East Coast band would really have a whole lot of following out here. But the place was *really* buzzing. There was just a really cool energy there. Once the show started, I was just sold. Those two hours were stellar. Little did I know that was going to turn into a life-changing night, but it did."

A big part of that life-changing experience had to do with the energy Adams found at the show, both onstage and within the crowd. "I'd seen Pearl Jam and Green Day and Stone Temple Pilots—bands like that. And the shows were usually sort of a loud, raucous party with everyone concentrating on getting drunk and throwing one another around. And, yeah, that's all well and good, but once I stood there in the crowd at Berkeley and heard the music, I was floored. There's a violin and a saxophone onstage, and that's pretty darn rare these days; who does that? And as DMB played, what I heard from them collectively just blew my mind. I stood there slack-jawed through a couple of their songs, like, 'Wow, who knew these instruments could all sound so good together?' And you just knew that the band was having a good time on top of it, which, in turn, made everybody in the crowd just feed off that. It's the kind of thing that you really can't explain. There was a whole bunch of us there that were seeing the band for the first time. But I was amazed at how many people knew every word and how much the crowd was playing off the band and knew the counts on different songs. I was like, 'Wow, this is kind of amazing.' There's only a couple bands in my life who have made me feel like, 'Man, I'm at home. This is a blast!' And DMB is one of them. I've spent many of my happiest moments at their shows."

Having made significant headway on the national scene by September 1995, DMB was back in the Bearsville Studio with Steve Lillywhite to begin work on what is considered to be the second of the Big Three, the band's sophomore album, *Crash.* Once again, DMB had several songs from its preexisting live stable to pull from, some of which (such as "Tripping Billies" and "Two Step") were quite old by now. This time, however, the band did do some writing specifically for the album in the form of "Too Much," "Crash into Me," and "Deed is Done" (the last of which ultimately did not make the album cut).

Once again, Tim Reynolds recorded with the band, and together the six musicians created an album that, while still maintaining the DMB sound they had collectively created, was a bit more rollicking and in your face than its predecessor. According to Lillywhite, the differences between *Under the Table* and *Crash* were very much a conscious production decision. In an August 13, 2008, interview with NPR's *World Cafe*, Lillywhite explained, "I always feel when you do more than one album with an artist [it's important] to try and carry the audience on some sort of journey. So all the rules we had on the first album, I tried to break on [*Crash*]. On *Under the Table* we only used acoustic guitars. On [*Crash*] we decided to amp up the acoustic guitars to give it more of a rock feel. On the first album . . . I pared Carter down; on [*Crash*] I told him to go for it. [*Crash*] is a lot more robust album."

In its May 3, 1996, review of *Crash*, *Entertainment Weekly* wrote, "The band's top-flight musicianship doesn't hurt, either; these boys can play. Cock an ear to Boyd Tinsley's violin rave-up on 'Tripping Billies,' or sax man LeRoi Moore's mellifluous honking on '#41.' Then there's Matthews' voice: Otherworldly and elegantly elastic, it fosters the impression that this guy must be some sort of visionary . . . one of the nicest things about DMB's music is that its distinctive complexity serves as a virtual assurance against a flood of lame imitator bands." Also citing the band's musicianship, Stephen Thomas Erlewine of the allmusic website wrote of the album, "Fusing together folk-rock, worldbeat, jazz, and pop, the band is arguably the most musically adept of all their contemporaries."

As opposed to the gentle welcome that "The Best of What's Around" provided for *Under the Table and Dreaming, Crash* gets right down to business with "So Much to Say," as Matthews's solo vocals and acoustics quickly give way to a honking full-band crescendo. The album's sound was generally tighter and punchier than that of *Under the Table,* featuring a mixture of high-energy, infectious tunes such as "Too Much," "So Much to Say," "Drive In, Drive Out," and "Lie in our Graves." These were rounded out with more jazzy languid songs such as "Proudest Monkey," "Let You Down," and the beautifully flute-driven "Say Goodbye." And, of course, there was DMB's most successful single to date, "Crash into Me," a mellow yet catchy tune, which received enough airplay that it would have been difficult to find anyone who didn't know the song in the mid- to late '90s, DMB fan or not. Despite the fact that the days of grunge had passed and more folky jam music had permeated the airwaves through the work of bands such as Blues Traveler, Rusted Root, and Spin Doctors, the DMB sound was still somewhat offbeat. One fan, Travis Howe, remembers, "I was in seventh grade when I experienced the *Crash* album, and the music was so odd to me. It was different, and I remember being afraid to admit that I really liked it."

Once again, Dave's unique manner of translating emotions to highly relatable lyrics captured audiences and resonated with fans new and old. Andrea Diaz-Vaughn, eighteen years old at the time *Crash* was released, remembers, "At that point in my life I was making big decisions and trying to learn how to live in a newly adult world. As I was going through it all, *Crash* was all I wanted to listen to. It spoke to me and cleared my head—I just remember driving around and listening to it all the time. *Crash* is completely inextricable from my memories of that period of life. It was what I had to get me through stuff at the time. It's such a good album that fourteen years later I could fall in love with it all over again. Not to mention it was *fun*—going to the shows was just so much fun. It was a great time to be young and hang out."

Though DMB had already outgrown its hometown venues, it played what would prove to be its final Trax show when it returned to the venue (and played a second consecutive set at the connected Max nightclub) to celebrate *Crash* with a record release show on April 29, 1996. The following day, *Crash* released, going straight to the number two spot on *Billboard*. Singles from the album ("Too Much," "So Much to Say," "Two Step," "Crash into Me," and "Tripping Billies") kept the album on the charts for the next 104 weeks. Though Erlewine predicted in his review that *Crash* would "please fans, but not novices," he was proved wrong; just over two months after its release, RIAA certified *Crash* platinum and, when all was said and done, the album went on to sell more than seven million copies. Not only that, but *Crash* resulted in DMB's only Grammy win of fourteen nominations to date for 1997's Best Performance by a Duo or Group for "So Much to Say." (DMB also received two other nominations that year; "Too Much" was nominated for Best Rock Song [won by Tracey Chapman, "Give Me One Reason"] and Best Rock Album [won by Sheryl Crow, *Sheryl Crow*].)

Gone were the days of clubs, bars, and even auditoriums and theaters when DMB went on the road to promote *Crash* over the course of the summer and fall of 1996. It was now headlining major venues such as SPAC, the Meadows (Hartford, Connecticut), Darien Lake (Darien Center, New York), and Madison Square Garden (New York City). As had always been the case with DMB, things had a tendency to grow exponentially, and by the following summer not only was the band playing amphitheaters, but it was filling two-night stands at places like the 25,000-capacity Shoreline Amphitheatre (Mountain View, California) and 20,000-capacity Great Woods Center for the Performing Arts (Mansfield, Massachusetts).

Even at those big venues, DMB managed to create a sense of intimacy. One fan, Pete Paszkowsi, whose first concert was in Albany, New York, at Knickerbocker Arena on October 10, 1996, remembers, "There was one moment that I will never, ever forget, which is why I've been to more than a hundred shows since then. I left my seat to get a drink, and as I was walking out, DMB started playing 'Lie in Our Graves.' I didn't want to miss it, so I stopped to watch. I was as far away from the stage as you can possibly get, pretty high up in the arena. I just stood there and watched Boyd's solo and tears started coming down my face. All the lights were down, except for some blue lights shining on Boyd. It was unbelievable. I stood there by myself, shocked at what was happening and how I was feeling. I just knew this was it—I had to keep going and having this experience over and over again. I still get that feeling all the time. It never stops. If it did, I'd probably consider going to fewer shows, but it's just never happened—I feel that way all the time."

Although audiences grew bigger as more and more fans like Paszkowski became enraptured by the music, the sense of community instilled in the band's early days continued on and the chance to just hang out remained a large part of DMB's appeal. Now, though, rather than hanging out in bars and clubs, the socialization moved to venue parking lots, where fans would show up hours ahead of time to chat, listen to music, drink some beers, fire up the grill, and partake in pickup games of Frisbee or football. Tailgating was half the fun, and this was a crowd that would make a day of it, arriving in the lots as early as possible to gather together and have a good time. With a day of fun already behind them, all would begin to make their way into the venue for the main event as the sun began to lower. Bryan Narciso, who discovered the scene at the Jones Beach Theater show on June 9, 1996, explains the importance of the environment: "As a teen in the midnineties I lost my way and I was headed down a wrong path until I found DMB. I remember borrowing money from my older brother to go see DMB, to get away from my problems, and after that my life completely took a positive tone. From that weekend on, my life changed. I began touring with DMB, traveling, meeting so many close friends along the way, people I would have never met if it wasn't for this band. People who, since meeting on tour, we have vacationed together, gone to weddings, and truly found a purpose in life."

The popularity of *Crash* made the live shows even more of a draw, with new fans constantly coming on board after either hearing radio singles or being told by friends that this was a not-to-be-missed experience. For their part, preexisting fans loved nothing more than taking a "virgin" to his or her first show. Brad Adams remembers the general excitement of discovery that permeated the whole scene in the mid-'90s: "I just remember being so excited after my first show and thinking, This was so cool. I want to take other friends to go see them just the way my friend did for me. Once *Crash* came out in 1996 and DMB started to explode, other people started to say, 'Oh, yeah, I know that band, they're pretty cool.' We'd invite them to shows with us, and it was really cool to kind of induct people into our little club. I remember how every time I told someone new about DMB I would think back to how my friend told me, 'You've got to *experience* their music.' Because if you hear DMB on the radio or MTV they sound fun and goofy and you think, Wow, there's a lot of different music going on here. But once you see them live and see how much fun they're having, how they feed off one another and the crowd, it's an *experience,* it really is."

Although DMB was already a successful act by 1996, Bryan Narciso looks back on the years from 1996 to 1998 as a particularly exciting time to be around and credits this to the great sense of novelty that existed both onstage and in the crowd throughout those years. "Looking back from this perspective, the energy that the band had was a bit different back then. It was still so raw, even as they were becoming popular. Compared to now, I just think the band took more chances, they were a little bit younger. Because the fan base was still so young, you still had the people that were there from the Trax and Charlottesville days. The energy levels in 1996 through 1998 were high in terms of fan morale, fan energy, and people just generally dancing around and having a great time. The crowd had more energy, the band had more energy and took more chances, and I'm glad to say I was around to experience that era. I remember clinging to every word of every 'Two Step' intro Dave improvised. Every *single* word. I think as musicians DMB has probably gotten better because they've really honed their craft but, in terms of energy and rawness, you'd never knew what to expect back then."

As the band and crowd grew, technology progressed as well. The Minarets Digest mailing list was defunct by mid-1995, but it gave way to sites such as DMBML (started as a mailing list in 1996 and expanded into a website later that year), where fans would come to check out the latest and greatest news about DMB and engage in conversations on the message boards. Additionally, with the continued expansion of the Internet, more and more individual sites began popping up, either as a simple tribute to DMB or as a means of providing tape lists to generate potential trades.

Things were buzzing, and it seemed that there was no end in sight. On October 28, 1997, DMB answered the bootlegging market with its first official live release, *Live at Red Rocks 8.15.95*. Amy Casillas, whose first DMB show just happened to be that Red Rocks gig, remembers, "You didn't really know it was going to be a big deal at the time; it was just another concert. It was DMB's first time playing there as a headliner, though they had opened for other bands at Red Rocks before. They opened with 'Seek Up,' and it felt like one giant song from 'Seek Up' to 'Warehouse,' which was about ten songs in. The crowd was really cool, and it felt like everyone was my age (I was in my early twenties at the time). We were just all into it, and I felt like I fit in with everyone around me." By the time Casillas saw DMB at Red Rocks two years later in 1997, it was a totally different scene. "DMB went from one night in 1995 to two completely sold-out nights in 1997. Almost everyone went to both nights, and it was turning into more of a *thing* to go to shows. Boyd was the star that night. I couldn't have even told you what Dave looked like for the first few years I saw the band. I remember telling my boyfriend during one of Boyd's solos that I swore he was vibrating—he was just on fire, it was so crazy. I remember being totally blown away."

As was becoming the norm, once again the band had a hit on its hands with *Live at Red Rocks*. Just over a month later, the album was certified platinum, debuting at number three on *Billboard* and remaining on the charts for the next thirty-six weeks, despite the fact that the album had been released without the benefit of any marketing or promotion.

Though the release gave a broader audience outside taping and trading circles the opportunity to hear DMB live, it also, once again, gave the taping and trading community pause. There was some worry that the band's officially released live recordings would affect—or even bring an end to—the taping policy altogether in an effort to ensure the live series market. But DMB's management took a gamble that the taper pulls and live recordings could coexist. DMB's willingness to test the market worked in its favor; official live recordings continued to be released and sold while trading marched on, proving that DMB fans' voracious appetite for music left enough room for both types of live show recordings. Matt Yette comments, "Imagine if they went ahead and said, 'Okay, we're going to put out *Live Trax* now and that's the end of taping.' They haven't done that. Not a lot of companies make the right decision—one that makes them money *and* makes the fans happy. And I think DMB has done both to an extreme degree by just kind of staying out of the way." Bill Lakenan adds that official releases and taper pulls "are not mutually exclusive, and I think at first everyone thought they would be. Nobody really knew how selling music on the Web was going to go. It's been an interesting path."

The release of *Live at Red Rocks* also expanded DMB's draw once again. Many who were already aware of DMB through its studio albums and radio airplay came to find that the same songs live offered a completely different energy from their studio-recorded counterparts. In his review of the album for allmusic, Stephen Thomas Erlewine opined, "*Live at Red Rocks 8.15.95* shouldn't disappoint fans already familiar with the band's loose-limbed, jazzy live show, but it should come as a revelation to listeners unacquainted with that aspect of Matthews." Erlewine was right. Introduced to DMB through this CD, one fan, Daniel Gardner, remembers the profound effect the music had on him at first listen. "My roommate was playing *Live at Red Rocks* in our apartment. From the moment I first heard 'Two Step,' I felt a rush come over my body that I had only ever felt before with a synthetic upper. I had found my new drug of choice, and it gave me a sweeter, fuller, longer-lasting high than I had ever experienced on anything—DMB was pure bliss. With those first notes of Dave and Boyd battling on guitar and violin, into the full crescendo of amazing drum beats laid by Carter, I have never heard anything like it!"

At the end of 1997, the band began recording its third album, *Before These Crowded Streets.* Rounding out the Big Three, *Before These Crowded Streets* was the final album before the hailstorm *The Lillywhite Sessions* (see chapter 5) left in its wake and the final chapter of the period throughout which the majority of fans regarded DMB and its music as fairly infallible.

Once again DMB went into the studio with producer Steve Lillywhite and guitarist Tim Reynolds, but there were several differences this time around. The band moved production out to the other side of the country, recording at Sausalito, California's Plant Recording Studio (also the birthplace of albums by Aretha Franklin, Stevie Nicks, and Journey), with final mixing completed in New York City. This time, having moved through most of their preexisting catalog previously with *Under the Table* and *Crash*, the majority of the album was not written prior to recording, though there were a few exceptions. "Leave Me Praying," which the band had been playing live throughout 1997, eventually morphed into the album's lead single, "Don't Drink the Water"; "Halloween," which had been in existence since 1992, was laid down as a recording for the first time (notably, a far more mellow recording than its live counterpart); and "Pig" had been played infrequently since its 1995 debut at Yoshi's in its earlier incarnation of "Don't Burn the Pig."

Certainly, for some, *Before These Crowded Streets* was a bit jarring upon its release. Compared to previous DMB albums, *Before These Crowded Streets* featured a more experimental band with more complex songs and more structure, featuring little interludes between several of the tracks, tying them into a cohesive story of sorts. This period marked a creatively ripe time for DMB, as its members wrote songs such as "Dreaming Tree," "The Stone," and "The Last Stop," all of which certainly sit atop many fans' lists of songs they most want to see live more than a decade later. Presumably, the combination of the differences in the songwriting process and the band's now-solid mainstream reputation made for an album that, while still retaining the DMB sound, was quite different from its predecessors. Though the eclecticism that marked earlier albums was still present with a wide range of sounds, from the Middle Eastern vibe of "The Last Stop" to the dreamy, floating riffs of "Spoon," *Before These Crowded Streets* had far more cohesion than earlier albums, in large part due to the snippet interludes that in many cases flowed one song into the next. The album also featured a much larger cast than DMB had brought into the studio previously, with Alanis Morissette providing guest vocals on

"Don't Drink the Water" and "Spoon"; the Kronos Quartet on "The Stone" and "Halloween"; Béla Fleck on "The Last Stop," "Don't Drink the Water," and "Spoon"; the Lovely Ladies on "Stay (Wasting Time)"; and the Charlottesville musicians Butch Taylor and John D'earth on "Rapunzel" and "Halloween," respectively.

With more fans than ever before by the time *Before These Crowded Streets* was released, anticipation for the album's April 28, 1998, release ran high. One fan, Anne Chatfield, recalls, "I played hooky from work in order to surprise my friend at her house so that we could go purchase the CD together first thing in the morning. I remember the anticipation on the car ride over to Tower Records as to what this new release was all about; this was before the days when songs were leaked out prerelease, so I had no idea what to expect. We went to get the CD and then promptly put it in the portable CD player in the car and went on a long drive. One of my first thoughts about *Before These Crowded Streets* is that it was sort of dark and Dave's voice seemed deeper than it had on previous albums. It's one of my favorite CDs to this day. Every time I walk into a show, I have a mental list of songs that I want to hear and jam out on with on my air violin, and twelve years later, many of the songs are still from *Before These Crowded Streets*."

On the credit of anticipation like Chatfield's, *Before These Crowded Streets* shot straight to the number one slot on *Billboard* upon its release, selling just under a half-million copies in its first week alone and going triple platinum by 1999 after remaining on the charts for eighty-nine weeks. Not only was *Before These Crowded Streets* nominated for two Grammys in 1998 (with "Crush" up for Best Pop Performance and *Before These Crowded Streets* up for Best Rock Album), but, as a testament to how much DMB had come to permeate the music landscape, "Crash into Me" from their previous album was simultaneously nominated for Best Rock Vocal. (Those three awards ultimately went to Jamiroquai ["Virtual Insanity" for Best Pop Performance]; John Fogerty [*Blue Moon Swamp* for Best Rock Album]; and the Wallflowers ["One Headlight" for Best Rock Vocal].

Though it took some fans a while to get used to the somewhat different *Before These Crowded Streets* sound, critics tended to favor it. On allmusic, Stephen Thomas Erlewine wrote, "The Dave Matthews Band made their reputation through touring, spending endless nights on the road improvising. Often, their records hinted at the eclecticism and adventure inherent in those improvisations, but *Before These Crowded Streets* is the first album to fully capture that adventurous spirit. Not coincidentally, it's their least accessible record, even if it's more of a consolidation than it is a step forward. Early Dave Matthews albums were devoted to the worldbeat fusions of *Graceland* and Sting, but his RCA efforts incorporated these influences into a smoother, pop-oriented style. Here, everything hangs out. Old trademarks, like jittery acoustic grooves and jazzy chords, are here, augmented by complex polyrhythms, Mideastern dirges, and on two tracks, the slashing strings of the Kronos Quartet. Some fans may find the new, darker textures a little disarming at first, but they're a logical extension of the group's work, and in many ways, this sonic daring results in the most rewarding album they've yet recorded." Anthony DeCurtis of *Rolling Stone* agreed, writing in the April 28, 1998, issue, "DMB is more successful on this outing than ever before in translating the roiling energy of its stage show to the studio. The band also pushes in adventurous new directions, incorporating bright new hues into its highly distinctive, instantly recognizable sonic palette."

Ironically, it is the song that *didn't* appear on this album that has arguably gone on to earn the most infamy among those well versed in all things DMB: "Mac Head." A photograph of the track listing for *Before These Crowded Streets* made its way to the public through an image included in DMB's 1999 calendar and "Mac Head" was on that list. The list was far from final, with songs that ultimately went on to make the *Before*

These Crowded Streets cut called by different names during their birthing process (for example, "The Last Stop" was referred to by the working title "Egyptian"). One song appeared on that list, however, that did *not* go on to appear on that album, and that song was "Mac Head." Lillywhite has acknowledged the existence of "Mac Head," describing it as a mix of Paul McCartney and Radiohead—thus the working "Mac Head" title. For years, fans attempted to procure a copy of this song through trading circles and message boards and debated whether or not it had morphed into a different, already known song along the way. All of this speculation has for the most part been to no avail. When asked about "Mac Head," band members have historically been somewhat evasive, leading people to believe for a time that "Mac Head" never actually existed in the first place.

In 2009, Jake Vigliotti joined the ranks of the presumably extremely select few who have actually had the opportunity to listen to "Mac Head." In a column written for antsmarching.org on November 7, 2009, Vigliotti revealed that he could confirm that "Mac Head" did, in fact, exist. By the time a secret source offered Vigliotti the chance to listen to it, the legend of this song had grown so great that Vigliotti was willing to make the drive from Florida to New York for the sole purpose of listening to "Mac Head," since the source was unwilling to distribute a recorded copy. Of the experience, Vigliotti says, "It was surreal. I got to the place to listen to 'Mac Head,' and literally five minutes later the song was playing. It was so nonchalant, like, 'Oh, that's "Mac Head."' The whole time I was driving [from Florida to New York] I was thinking, this is so stupid. I mean, I've heard other songs that weren't released—there's a reason they're not released: they suck. So I heard 'Mac Head' and thought, that song's not bad, actually. It's got a nice sort of rhythm to it. I like this. And I heard it again, then heard another take of it and thought, this song's got some potential. Just put some different lyrics here, and you've got it. It was weird. It was worth the drive. I don't know if it was worth it to my wife and kids, but it was cool to me."

For Vigliotti, the road to "Mac Head" was much longer than just the I-95 corridor from Florida to New York. "The song's been known about since 1999, and literally since that time I've been bugging everyone possible about it. Everyone. I've talked to people close to the band. One guy told me, 'No, it's not real. It's an inside joke. I listened to the tapes, it's not there.' And I was crushed. Then I talked to another guy, who said, 'It was really, really early, like in November 1997, and they just never brought it back.' Then Boyd mentioned it. Then a reporter did an interview with Dave and e-mailed me beforehand and said, 'If you could ask Dave about anything, what would it be?' So I told him to ask about 'Mac Head.' He asked Dave about it, and Dave almost fell out of his chair, then said, 'We've recorded a lot of songs. I don't remember them all.' I felt like I was so close to getting an answer. So when this opportunity popped up, I thought, I've gotta do this. I've gotta get up there and hear this song. It has sort of a little 'Sleep to Dream Her' [*Everyday*] part in it. I honestly thought it wasn't gonna be any good. I thought this was the stupidest thing I could ever do. But I'd gone that far, I couldn't quit until I heard it."

Though DMB never played "Mac Head" before an audience, it hit the road hard for the remainder of 1998 to promote the songs that did make the *Before These Crowded Streets* cut. For the first time, in addition to the large amphitheaters DMB was already frequenting, stadiums were added into the mix, including one night each at the 60,000-plus-capacity Foxboro Stadium (Foxborough, Massachusetts) and 80,000-capacity Giants Stadium (East Rutherford, New Jersey). The June 5, 1998, Foxboro show was a night of firsts, marking not only DMB's first headlining show but also the first appearance of the Lovely Ladies onstage to provide live backing vocals for "Stay (Wasting Time)," as well as a guest appearance by the South African penny whistle player "Big Voice" Jack on several songs, including "One Sweet World," "#36," and "Dreaming Tree." In addition to the stadium crowd in attendance, thousands of others watched the show live through a VH1 live broadcast of the first few songs. One fan, Mark "Cali" Calandrello, who attended the Foxboro show, remembers being overwhelmed by the whole experience. "I remember walking into the stadium and just being in awe at the amount of people. The stage was so big, there really wasn't a bad seat in the house. Just being around so many people and hearing them all sing together with the band—it was definitely a very powerful experience."

In addition to the music, the sense of communal celebration helped draw even more fans into the fold. One fan, Brenda Gonzalez, remembers being overwhelmed by the awesome spectacle of it all during her first DMB show at the Great Western Forum in Inglewood, California, in 1998. "Not knowing what to expect, I was a little bit disoriented. I remember thinking, Oh my God, all these people are crazy. The crowd was just going insane for every song. But then I remember realizing on the parts where the whole crowd really pitches in and almost *becomes* part of the band, This is awesome. I really want to be a part of this. It was just such a good feeling to be in there and part of this totally unique thing with all these people."

Despite the fact that DMB was now an indisputable heavy hitter on the music scene, it operated as usual, continuing to foster a very real sense of a relationship with their fans. Of course, as is the case with any band of DMB's caliber, most fans have never met a band member face-to-face. That does not, however, take away from the sense of solidarity or commitment the vast majority of fans feel with and to the band. In addition to DMB's musical prowess and relatable lyrics, which many fans cite as "therapeutic" and "the sound track of my life," it's likely that the band members' Everyman attitude has a lot to do with this sense of unity and accessibility. Despite the fact that DMB could now easily pack tens of thousands of fans into amphitheaters at each stop, in so many ways the band continued to appear to be professional musicians as opposed to inaccessible rock stars. Unlike many other bands that pull large crowds into big venues, DMB proved to have the knack of creating a sense of intimacy even in settings that were anything but. Every night the band sauntered onstage quietly, looking around and taking in the roaring, jubilant crowd before picking up their instruments and lighting the room on fire. Once the music began, DMB appeared to be having just as much of a celebration as the crowd around them, with Dave's jittering movements and Carter's wide grin peeking out from behind his massive drum kit. One fan, Jeff Cunningham, explains his take on the experience: "There's this wonderful bond between the band members and the fans. If you whittle away at the onion, it's not even about the music anymore. It's about the human beings involved in this experience and all the love shooting back and forth between the stage and the crowd."

DMB fans continued to be industrious outside show settings as well. Although grassroots promotion was no longer necessary, fans remained avid in their continued promotion of and loyalty to DMB, spreading tapes and talking up the band and its music as though it were still critical to the success of DMB. One fan, Jeanette Coppola Balkiewicz, explains that it was a display of such deep-seated passion that made her take a second listen to DMB and that has shaped her life ever since. "I was hanging with my friend Mike in his room, and he was wearing a DMB T-shirt and listening to *Under the Table and Dreaming*. Now, it's not like I hadn't heard this album yet—I actually owned it by this time. But on this night, I heard it in a different way. Mike was so passionate about this album and this band that it became infectious to me. I had a yearning to feel what he felt. I immediately went home, listened, and then the next day went to the mall to buy *Remember Two Things* and *Crash*. I will forever thank Mike for this gift, which has transformed my life."

1998 saw the birth of nancies.org, which would become the biggest online gathering hub for fans yet and the go-to spot for checking out the latest and greatest news about DMB and engaging in conversations on the message boards. One of the most prominent DMB websites to date, nancies.org reflected the tendencies of the fan base even in its creation. According to cofounder John Athayde, a collection of about a dozen fans from various locations across the country came together remotely, combining their efforts to create a comprehensive website. Up to this point, even the DMB official website did not include set lists and other information fans were looking for. With the birth of nancies.org, all this was suddenly available in an organized, easily accessible form. Jeanette Coppola Balkiewicz remembers the draw of nancies.org for fans like herself: "I started meeting such wonderful people who shared the same love. I was seventeen at the time, and I was talking to people of all ages; no one cared how old you were. It was amazing to me how accepting the community was. Before I knew it, I was trading tapes. It was such a joyous time for me. I had become someone who finally found a passion. And not only that, but I found other people who shared the same passion. I was in Heaven." Additionally, the message board format allowed for more of a dynamic, real-time conversation—and also for more people to participate. Jake Vigliotti comments, "I think for the online community, things really took off when the mailing lists turned into websites—like with DMBML.com and nancies.org. I'd go online, and that's how I kept up with the band. I'd go on to try to find someone to tape trade with or to read up on the news." Nancies.org (affectionately referred to as "the CNN of DMB" by Matt Yette) had such a huge draw that it won the VH1 award for Coolest Fan Web Site in 2001.

The DMB crowd has always been an Internet-savvy bunch, and for many these message boards became a way of life. The intensity of community members meant that even when the band was off the road and not receiving lots of national airtime on radio stations, DMB remained at the top of their minds. Whether the band was touring or not, the community remained in close touch. Trading tapes, debating what would come next for the band, reminiscing about old shows, and making plans for upcoming tours—all of these things were fodder for conversation, and thus DMB was a part of daily life.

DMB did its part in promoting this ongoing sense of community by opening the official Warehouse fan club in December 1998. For thirty dollars a year, fans could sign up for a membership that included advance ticket sales, limited-release recordings, members-only website access, and potential opportunities to meet band members and receive ticket upgrades. According to a Warehouse statement, the underlying notion behind the club was "to foster greater interaction between the band and our loyal friends." Most enticing to fans (and especially those who were frequent showgoers) was the opportunity to avoid long lines at ticket outlets and the potential to secure better seats based on the Warehouse's seniority system. Over the years, those 1998 and 1999 Warehouse memberships have become a valuable commodity as thousands and thousands more fans have joined and original members' seniority has become more coveted. Although exact membership numbers are unknown, a February 1, 2007, article in *Fast Company* stated that there were upward of 80,000 Warehouse members at the time of publication. In terms of how the fan club affected ticket sales, an April 22, 2002, article in *The Wall Street Journal* reported that in the example of a 17,000-seat arena, 8,000 tickets had been sold directly through the Warehouse.

One fan, Mike Leone, who joined the Warehouse the day after it opened in December 1998, remembers how much it changed things. "What it's done for me is priceless. Warehouse was one of the first, if not *the* first, subscription club to offer fans specific benefits. At that time they opened, you're talking a few thousand members, so when they did ticket sales you were guaranteed the first ten rows center for anything you ordered. In the early days, the Warehouse would give all the summer tour dates at once and post confirmations a week or two before public on-sale, as opposed to the day before public on-sale like they generally do now.

They would also post seat locations at the same time as your tickets were confirmed. Today they've tightened things up because of scalpers, but there was a time when you would put in for tickets and know your seat location within the month.

"Someone like me joined in December 1998, and for *twelve* years, I've never had to deal with Ticketmaster. That in and of itself is amazing. When I bought tickets for my first show in '96, we had to go stand outside Dominic's and wait for doors to open to buy tickets from Ticketmaster. At that point it all came down to who was going to camp out the longest. Then this little website comes along and I don't have to camp out, I don't have to call Ticketmaster's 800 number from two different phones in my house—because, remember, no one really had cell phones in '98. What the Warehouse has saved me just in headaches alone over the years is immeasurable. When Warehouse opened, people were paying to avoid dealing with Ticketmaster. People join today more in the hopes they'll end up in the front row."

In many ways, the Warehouse would go on to revolutionize band-fan relationships across the music industry. Eventually, Coran Capshaw started Musictoday, a company that ultimately managed more than two hundred heavy-hitting acts and provided them with a template to communicate more directly with their fans, much as DMB had. In line with the Warehouse model, this often worked through the management of direct-to-fan sales, presale ticket offers, and specialized merchandise. (In 2006, Live Nation bought out Musictoday.)

In addition to all of the other activity buzzing around DMB, tape trading was evolving quickly as CD-burning technology became more and more mainstream. Even as DMB grew into a more renowned band, achieving commercial success and building its library of official studio releases, trading marched on. In fact, in many ways it gathered even *more* momentum as time went by and the exponentially multiplying fan base got in on music sharing and show collecting. To some degree, tapes still spread the music to new fans, but, most notably, they played the greater function of solidly uniting the increasingly large fan base, continuing to provide a good reason for fan-to-fan interaction, and ensuring that fans could enjoy an incessant stream of new material.

Moreover, because DMB happened to come around at a time of rapid-fire technological advancement, trading and copying music became an easier and less time-consuming process, thus opening the practice to a greater number of people. More widespread Internet access led to the rise of message boards (most notably nancies.org and DMBML) in lieu of mailing lists, where fans could congregate to request and locate trades in real-time. Finding shows became a simpler process as people began to post their show lists online, both on message boards and on their personal websites.

As the years went by, cassettes fell out of vogue and DMB traders, like the rest of the world, moved on to the CD format. According to Andy Svenson, it was at that time that many DMB fans, sensing that cassettes were never to return, began getting rid of their tape collections, handing entire cassette libraries over to interested parties in one fell swoop. As a result of this format change, over time many of the early-'90s cassette recordings became difficult to track down. Even the traders who *did* have the foresight to transfer their cassettes to CD format did not necessarily end up with clear copies of the older recordings due to the new, not-yet-perfected technology of CD burning.

Along with this, recording technology improved. More sophisticated recording gear at a more affordable price (though still not cheap) meant that tapers were acquiring better-quality show recordings as the years went by. Although strict rules for preserving the integrity of the music throughout the course of trading remained in effect, CDs did not lose quality over the generations as tapes did.

As the 1990s came to an end, DMB and its fan base found themselves in an enviable position. Here was a rare example of a band that had indisputably made waves in the mainstream music scene while still managing to maintain and significantly grow a fan base that sustained the sort of fervor and dedication that is rarely found outside independent acts. All the while, DMB's songwriting withstood the pressures that come with recording for major record labels, and longtime fans continued to find the band compelling. As Steve Lillywhite explained, "I think fans really did come on this journey with us through those three albums." The community, for its part, continued to grow closer and maintain its common identity, despite its rapidly increasing numbers. As the 1990s closed, it seemed as though things couldn't have been going better if they had been scripted.

From Hard-Core Fan to Heavy-Hitting DJ

Mark "Cali" Calandrello started out like an average DMB fan. A college student in 1998, he went to his first concert at Foxboro Stadium in Foxborough, Massachusetts, with a big group of friends. For Cali, it was love at first sight, despite his somewhat measured expectations. Cali says, "When I went to my first show, it was more so because it was the thing to do—I was not expecting it to be what it was. After going to the show I just fell in love. It was the most *amazing* time. I'm just really all about being with my friends, having a good time, and, as cheesy as this sounds, I just love to sing and dance." Sold after his first show, Cali and his friends started hitting up DMB's Boston and Hartford shows whenever they came through.

Meanwhile, Cali was also working his way up the ranks at Boston's now-defunct rock station and CBS affiliate 104.1 WBCN, covering a variety of different events, music-related and otherwise. It was in the early 2000s that he was assigned to on-air promotion for the X Games. While working on this project, Cali's point person happened to ask him if he was a DMB fan, to which Cali responded, "Yeah, to be perfectly honest, they're my favorite band." As luck would have it, it happened that this point person was affiliated with DMB. "And the rest," as Cali says, "is history."

Through his DMB contact, in 2001 Cali had his first opportunity to interview Stefan Lessard for WBCN while the bass player and winter sports enthusiast was doing an appearance at the Rossignol booth for an annual ski show held at Boston's Bayside Expo. Cali remembers, "I went down, did the interview, posted it online, and it kind of took off from there. I think the fans really enjoyed it because here was a radio guy asking fan-type questions—not generic stuff like 'Do you wear boxers or briefs?' We did it again, and it kind of became a yearly ritual to do these interviews. I think the fans like it because it's from a fan point of view and because Stefan and I really became good friends to where I think people feel like it's listening in on someone's conversation at this point. I've interviewed him a bunch of times now, and I love interviewing him more than anyone else because of that rapport we have."

Indeed, over the years, Cali has gained quite a reputation within the DMB community, and his annual interviews with Stefan and other band members not only are featured on CBS radio website, but are also archived on DMB fan sites such as antsmarching.org and dontburnthepig.org.

In addition to Stefan, Cali has had face time with Dave and Boyd. "During that first interview with Dave back in 2003, I got to ask him a bunch of questions that I don't think he was expecting, like 'What's in the silver mug that you drink onstage?' But Dave can kind of—in a *good* way—go off and take a question and make it a six-minute answer. Which is great, but then the interview is over. I really like interviewing Stefan the most because I think he's the most real person. He's just so unbelievably *normal*. You don't look at him like he's in the biggest band in the world."

The key to his successful interviews with Stefan and other band members, Cali says, is thinking like a fan. "When I interview Stefan, I just really ask the questions that I want to know and I think it's the same questions the fans want to know. It doesn't take me long to come up with these questions. For this last interview I just sat down and wrote them out in about two minutes."

THE ALBUM THAT WASN'T

OUT OF MY HANDS

When it came time for DMB's next studio album, things had heated to a fever pitch. Every time it seemed like things couldn't get any bigger—they did. As far as most people were concerned, there was no stopping this band, either onstage or in the studio; after nearly a decade, it had yet to falter. But despite the fact that DMB's future seemed certain, it continued to tour like a band that had something to prove.

It seemed as though every time you turned around, a new DMB tour was beginning: 1998 saw it tour almost constantly from May through December (including a midsummer European run that had DMB opening for the Rolling Stones at several gigs). Even when the band wasn't on tour, Dave continued playing on his own, remaining on the road for most of the winter of 1999 for some more intimate acoustic shows with friend and sometime collaborator Tim Reynolds while DMB was on break.

Come summertime 1999, the demand for DMB spiraled to even higher levels. Not only was the band playing multiple nights at large amphitheaters, but more and more stadiums were added to the schedule as well. That summer saw three nights at the Philadelphia Veterans Stadium (65,000-plus capacity), two nights at Giants Stadium, and two nights at Foxboro. DMB ended the year with the third-highest-grossing tour of the year (and the thirty-second-highest-grossing tour of all time in North America)—just behind the legendary touring powerhouses the Rolling Stones and Bruce Springsteen. According to Billboard.com, there was a huge leap forward in not only audience size but (predictably) touring revenue from 1998 to 1999, with DMB's annual touring gross increasing from $26 million to $44.5 million in just twelve months' time. It seemed the band couldn't get any higher, that they could do no wrong. But, of course, what goes up . . .

Following a few months of recuperation, in winter 2000 DMB went back into the studio for round four with producer Steve Lillywhite. By this time, the band had purchased its own studio, Haunted Hollow, in Charlottesville, marking the first time DMB would remain home while recording. According to Lillywhite in the 2009 documentary *The Road to Big Whiskey,* this was mistake number one for the band. "It's very different recording in your hometown. When you go away, you're going away to make a record. When you're recording in your hometown, you're going to work."

There were other problems with the recording location as well. While the actual location and many details of Haunted Hollow studio are not publicly discussed (to protect the band's privacy), the band members all agreed that the studio as it appeared in that winter of 2000 was not conducive to creativity and excitement. According to Lessard, "It felt suffocating writing music in that studio. We've actually built that studio out since *The Lillywhite Sessions* and now it's an actual real studio. But when we were working [on that album], it was a dance hall with a low ceiling.

There were no lights, everyone had headphones on, so you had canned head all day and you were walking around and you're all grumpy . . . for six months."

Whereas most of the band's previous recording sessions had occurred fairly quietly, the rapid rise of technology, more widespread use of computers, and increasingly avid nature of the band's online following changed all of that this time around. Throughout the recording of this fourth album (which fans would title *The Lillywhite Sessions;* it was also known alternately as *The Summer So Far*, though the latter designation was used primarily by media outlets such as *Rolling Stone*), leaks were the norm rather than the exception. Message boards (primarily DMBML and nancies.org) were littered with information about song titles and other studio happenings—details that were filtering out in real time. While much of this news turned out to be illegitimate, some of it was not. In fact, Lillywhite even shared some information on the latest and greatest studio happenings through fan websites. Additionally, clips made their way to the Internet via insiders and Red Light Management itself.

This whole scenario was a new (and frankly unsettling) one for the band. With previous albums such as *Under the Table and Dreaming* and *Crash,* the majority of tracks had already been known by the fan base. Although some of them certainly sounded different in the studio, fans had a general idea of what to expect. In the case of *Before These Crowded Streets,* leaks simply didn't happen, presumably in large part because DMB was recording away from home (and, therefore, with fewer "insiders" around) and because the Internet had not yet advanced to the point it did just a couple years later. But by the time *The Lillywhite Sessions* was recorded, technology and fan anticipation were more powerful than ever before.

While the band's fans were chomping at the bit for any tidbits of new songs from the new album, there were murmurs of dissent and dissatisfaction in the Charlottesville studio. The recording process dragged on for six months, and although fans mostly liked what they heard through the various clips and snippets that infiltrated the Internet, there were hints that something was a little bit "off" with the band. Dave's lyrics were particularly dark, and though he had never steered a wide circle around heavy topics such as death and loss, *The Lillywhite Sessions* seemed to fixate on that darkness. The levity and hope that generally counterbalanced such heavier topics were simply not coming through. Though this may not have been a problem for the fans who were hearing improvised versions of the lyrics, it made for an arduous, plodding recording process for the band.

Finally, in June 2000, Red Light Management announced that the album—originally expected to release that summer—would be pushed back. DMB would break from recording to do its annual tour and resume studio work once the summer dates were over. Though the record company wanted an album, this wasn't necessarily seen as the end of the world among fans. DMB had built its reputation on working songs out in front of audiences before committing them to the studio, so their fans were eager to hear some of the new tunes live during that summer's tour. Indeed, the tour attendees *did* get a taste of the new album that summer in the form of "Sweet Up and Down," "Grey Street," "Digging a Ditch," "Bartender," "JTR," "Grace Is Gone," "Raven," and "Busted Stuff" (initially introduced to fans as "She My Bitch").

The tour was, once again, a big one. Unbelievably, the crowds were still getting bigger, with even more stadiums (Soldier Field in Chicago and Three Rivers Stadium in Pittsburgh) added to those from 1998 and 1999 and additional nights tacked onto Giants Stadium, which now hosted the band for a three-night stand. When all was said and done, DMB was officially the number one touring act in America during 2000.

Nate Vandemark, who first saw DMB play at small northeast bars and at Trax, remembers those Giants Stadium shows in 2000 as the time when he consciously stopped, took it all in, and realized how big DMB and its fan base had become. "I remember just looking around, and something about that night—I don't know what it was, maybe they did something that reminded me of Trax or something—but I remember looking around at the sixty-five thousand other people around me and thinking how lucky I was. For a few good minutes, I just felt this very real sense of how lucky I was to have had the opportunity to see DMB play such small places previously. It was just so surreal to know that I had seen them when no one knew who they were—and the next thing you know, they're selling out three nights at Giants Stadium. That was a trip."

Mike Leone also remembers that time as one of expansion. "It was hard not to notice. I was going from seeing them in a not-sold-out World Music Theater (in Tinley Park, Illinois) to seeing them at Soldier Field (in Chicago, Illinois), which was selling out two nights in a row. It was actually kind of fun. To me it meant that the band I had been passionate about for so long was successful—I now got to follow an even bigger band.

"What ended up happening, though," he continues, "is that there was definitely a bit of a shift—it went from people following DMB because it was cool to follow the music around to it being cool because you just wanted to say you were at the show." Leone wasn't sure if the new attendees were merely scenesters or true fans of the band and the music. "To me, it was just a period of time, the growth curve. You go up, and eventually you hit a peak and then you come down a little bit. True fans will want to stay with you for the whole ride."

Things were expanding onstage as well. Charlottesville native and keyboardist Butch Taylor (who had formerly played in Secrets with Carter and LeRoi, had contributed keys on *Before These Crowded Streets,* and had joined the band for a few dates during the 1998 and 1999 tours) became a staple that summer of 2000. Despite his new status with DMB, Taylor technically actually represented a return to the band's roots—it had, after all, begun its career with Griesar on keyboards. Post-2000 DMB rarely played with only the five founding members onstage.

By the time DMB got off the road in September 2000, online rumors were spreading that Steve Lillywhite was going to be dropped from the recording sessions. By now accustomed to the songs that had come from these sessions and to Lillywhite himself as an integral piece of the recording puzzle, the rumors didn't seem all that credible to most fans. On September 9, 2000, nancies.org noted, "Rumors have been flying around Nancies and other discussion groups for a few weeks that producer Steve Lillywhite (DMB's studio producer since 1996's *Crash*) has been fired from working with the band. None of the rumors was especially convincing, and we'd written them off as mere fiction. But now those rumors are running strong in Charlottesville. Though the band has kept mum, some of their local associates are anonymously confirming the rumor. It appears that it was less a firing and more of a parting of ways and differing of interests."

The rumors, it turned out, were right. On October 6, 2000, a message on the home page of the band's official website read, "Beginning Monday, October 9, Dave Matthews Band will re-enter the studio to begin recording their fourth studio album, this time with producer Glen Ballard." This was jarring news, and fans began to grow concerned that the songs that had already been laid down with Lillywhite would be scrapped. Pete Paszkowski remembers, "You started hearing things online about the band and what was going on—I remember feeling a bit nervous about it all. I wondered what they were going to do with all this beautiful music. There was also some nervousness in terms of what was going to happen to the band."

Although fans were confused as to why the sessions and the band's work with Lillywhite had been abandoned, Stefan Lessard says that after six months of tedious recording it was time for a change. "My A&R guy came on my bus when we were on tour. Carter and I were there, and he said, 'This isn't working. You guys aren't anywhere near done. It's been six months, it doesn't seem like anyone really wants to work with Lillywhite anymore. The band doesn't seem to be talking. We need to do something drastic. What do you think about trying a different producer for this next one?'"

"Well," Stefan explains, "I'm a student. I joined this band when I was sixteen and I was in high school—I sort of fell out of college and into this band. So *always* when I have the opportunity to do something new or work with someone new in this profession: *Yes!* Okay, we worked with Lillywhite for three records, that's great. Glen Ballard, he worked with Quincy Jones, and I'm a *huge* fan of Quincy Jones. I was like, 'Sure, great. We'll go to L.A.' They told us we had to be done in two months. 'Great! That's even better!' So, yeah, let's do it."

And so it was that Dave made a solo trip to L.A. to meet up with producer Glen Ballard, known for creating radio-friendly hits in the pop vein for major artists such as Alanis Morissette (*Jagged Little Pill*), No Doubt (*Return of Saturn*), and Wilson Phillips (*Wilson Phillips*). Whether right or wrong, if DMB fans consider there to be a villain in the DMB story, there's a big argument that title would go to Ballard.

Though it has been reported that Dave originally went to L.A. with the intention of writing a single song with Ballard, the two ended up writing an entire album of ten songs in just twelve days. The good news was that Dave had broken out of his dark songwriting rut. The more questionable news was that this album, *Everyday,* completely deviated from the typical DMB formula of collaborative songwriting efforts. Rather than improvising and creating songs as a complete or partial group either in the studio or onstage, by the time the balance of the band arrived in L.A. to record, their instrumental parts had already been written for them by Matthews and Ballard. As Boyd Tinsley explained in an April 17, 2002, interview with *Rolling Stone*, "We had sheet music going in, which we'd never had before. There were definitive parts laid down for us." While the quick recording process was likely a welcome relief from the six months of stagnancy that had plagued the *The Lillywhite Sessions* back in Charlottesville, this was a massive deviation from standard operating procedure.

Aside from the manner in which it was created, there were other significant differences between *Everyday* and its predecessors. For the first time, Dave plugged in, using an electric guitar on the majority of the album. Also, Glen Ballard's pop sensibilities were extremely apparent on *Everyday* tracks. Gone were the languid jams, intricate instrumental work, and emphasis on violin and horn that had set DMB's earlier albums apart from the pack. *Everyday* was straight to the point, far more mainstream than any other DMB album to date, and radio friendly, with most songs clocking in around the four-minute mark and no song longer than 4:43 ("Everyday"). In the end, *Everyday* sounded like a studio album. And although that is admittedly precisely what it was, unlike Lillywhite, Ballard did not infuse the live sensibility that so epitomized DMB—and that previous albums had always had—into this album.

Everyday featured Ballard on keyboards and piano and Carlos Santana's guitar work on the track "Mother Father." Every tune on the album was new and previously unknown to fans, with the exception of the song "Everyday," which was an evolution of "#36," in existence since 1993. When the first single, "I Did It," was released in January 2001, fans were shocked. Nothing could have been a more drastic shift from the known commodities of *The Lillywhite Sessions* than this short, punchy, upbeat, electric-driven single. Moreover, the sound was at the farthest end of the spectrum from the acoustic, instrumentally complex sound and weightier lyrics DMB fans had come to know and love in the course of the past decade.

While "I Did It," for better or worse, marked a turning point for DMB and its fans, it also marked a turning point for the music industry. On January 3, 2001, DMB made music history by being the first major label group to officially release a single on Napster. By that point, Napster (which served as the primary face of peer-to-peer music sharing at the time) had become a polarizing issue among musicians. Though the technology actually helped newer musicians get their sound out even without the benefit of a major distributor, more established musicians such as Metallica and Dr. Dre fought hard to preserve their copyrighted materials and potential lost earnings. Not only did DMB not take part in this fight, it adapted to the changing atmosphere by using Napster to its advantage in the promotion of its new single and album. As Matthews said in a March 2, 2001, article on MTV online, "I don't see the sense in fighting something that is the future. I don't feel that I'm in the position to say I'm being ripped off by Napster in any way."

A January 11, 2001, press release issued by Napster read, "By releasing the new single 'I Did It' via Napster, [Dave Matthews Band] has become the first major label act to do so with its label's permission. The band, which began offering the song on its own Web site last week, wanted its Napster-using fans to have a clean version of the song, since several poor-quality recordings of the tune that were taped off radio have surfaced on the service. DMB's publicist said, 'Dave Matthews Band was happy to hear of Napster users' enthusiasm for "I Did It," but wants to make certain that DMB fans listening to the song via the Internet also have access to a high-quality MP3 file that sounds as the band intended,' the group said in a statement issued Thursday (January 11).Visitors to the Napster Web site are greeted by a brief description of 'I Did It' and can search for the song by clicking on a link."

Although it would have been impossible to have the foresight to see where the music industry was headed when DMB began in 1991, it was in the rapidly evolving music landscape nearly a decade later that the band's taping and trading history and independent roots were turning out to be invaluable. Unlike other bands, which had taken more traditional routes to major-label success, DMB had an intimate understanding of the value of word of mouth and music sharing and because of this was far more capable and willing than the vast majority of its peers to shift with the changing tide of the music market.

Indeed, Napster and the other file-sharing sites that would follow in its wake had both a light and a dark side. Though DMB is most linked with the words "leak" and "Napster" based on events that would occur a bit later in 2001, in addition to the officially-released-to-Napster "I Did It" single, the rest of the tracks from *Everyday* leaked illegally prior to the album's February 27, 2001, release. In a March 7, 2001, Yahoo! News article, the writer Phil Gallo succinctly captured the (at the time) seemingly illogical way Napster worked, writing, "[*Everyday*] is the biggest debut and single week of sales for the year. The heavily marketed album, the DMB's seventh, has been driven by the single 'I Did It' over the last several weeks. To a certain degree, its success flies in the face of logic that says Napster exposure hurts record sales. The album's tracks have been illegally available through the file-sharing service for almost a month."

Once again, DMB's strategy and the reputation it had built paid off. *Everyday* released on February 27, 2001, with the biggest first-week sales DMB had yet seen. The album shot straight to number one, with 755,000 copies sold in the first week alone. Within six weeks it went double platinum, and by the end of the year, the album was certified triple platinum by the RIAA. *Everyday*'s second single, "The Space Between," was nominated for a Grammy for Best Rock Vocal Performance by a Duo or Group in 2002 (the Grammy ultimately went to U2 for "Elevation").

While *Rolling Stone*'s David Fricke wrote what was meant to be a very positive review of *Everyday,* it encapsulated exactly why this album was a smash with the more commercial market and a disappointment to the original fan community. "The opening riff is a crusty stutter of guitar that Creed would kill to copyright. A hydraulic piano groove is peppered with zesty sprays of strum and violin flutter. And the lyric hook in the chorus is just three tight syllables—'I did it'—jackhammered into your skull. The first single from the Dave Matthews Band's fourth studio album, *Everyday,* 'I Did It' is no-fat monster pop, the kind of hit that will dog you so hard for the next year—on radio, TV and especially barroom jukeboxes, where pickled jocks will bark along like the Molson Tabernacle Choir—that you'll think the song is a CIA tracking device. After a decade as one of America's hottest cult acts, able to sell out stadium tours with modest airplay, the Dave Matthews Band is about to go big—and 'I Did It' will be the tune that does it. This is not a bad thing. We're stuck in an age of dull extremes: teen-pop sugar zombies, the steel bawls and fake-blood theater of the new metal. It's so flat and dire in the Billboard Top Twenty that the long-gone Beatles whipped the competition silly for two months. Right now, the most radical and exhilarating thing a band can do is shoot right up the middle, dead center through the mainstream."

Compare this to a fan viewpoint as expressed in a column written for nancies.org, titled "Anyone Seen the Gong?": "An obvious question some of y'all are probably having is why I'm the first person on the nancies.org staff to comment on the album since its release on 27 February. This is because it's difficult to comment on. Basically, it sucks. No, it doesn't suck in relation to most of the recordings currently on the *Billboard 200.* It doesn't, honestly even really suck. But, in relation to what the Dave Matthews Band is capable of—or even what they've recorded previously—it's dreadful."

Of course, more moderate sentiments existed as well. Bryan Narciso remembers his view on *Everyday:* "When I heard *The Lillywhite Sessions* live, especially on the heels of *Before These Crowded Streets,* which I would probably say is my favorite album overall from top to bottom in terms of production and everything else, I really felt like DMB was most in line with what they were as a band. When I heard *Everyday* I *liked* it, but I felt like they were off course from what they really were. In terms of everything from reading about how it came about to Glen Ballard, from a fan perspective it just seemed like DMB took a different direction—and people don't like change. I remember the fans just crying out over *Everyday*. I didn't think it was bad, I didn't take it personally. You can't always write the same songs—how many times can Dave write 'Seek Up' as he gets older, as he has children? As fans, we forget that the person we look up to does grow up and change in their life as we do and it's never going to be the same."

While long-standing fans were wrapping their heads around this new-sounding DMB, the band's poppier sound and songs made for radio singles rendered them far more accessible than they had ever been. Commercially, the album was a success. But within fan circles, the already shocking sound of *Everyday* was exacerbated by the knowledge of what could have been with *The Lillywhite Sessions*. There was simply no comparing songs like "Fool to Think" and "Sleep to Dream Her" (*Everyday*) with "Bartender" and "Grey Street" (*The Lillywhite Sessions*).

As chance would have it, just a few weeks after *Everyday*'s release, in March 2001 DMB fans (and the world at large) *did* have the unanticipated chance to compare *Everyday* and *The Lillywhite Sessions* on a track-by-track basis. Through a somewhat complex (and, to this day, largely unknown) series of events, in March 2001 Craig Knapp, who was not only a DMB fan but also a member of the DMB tribute band Ants Marching, received a CD in the mail titled *The Summer So Far*. According to a July 9, 2001, *Rolling Stone* article on the whole series of events, Greg Heller wrote that the CD was accompanied by a note that read: "[This CD] is the Virginia album that was to be released last summer. The story of how this got out is sketchy and unreliable. I will spare you the story." Upon hearing the CD, Knapp knew that the lost tracks from *The Lillywhite Sessions* were in his possession.

Knapp now found himself in an ethical conundrum, which he shared with other fans on the message boards of DMBML. Dying to hear *The*

Lillywhite Sessions, many fans attempted to persuade Knapp to share the music, but he was not convinced that it was the right thing to do. Finally, he exchanged a series of e-mails with Steve Lillywhite, asking what he should do with the recordings now in his possession. Only, unbeknown to him, Knapp—who had been transparent about the whole process on the DMBML message boards—wasn't actually corresponding with Lillywhite at all but with a fan posing as Lillywhite. Not surprisingly, this fan-as-Lillywhite ultimately gave Knapp the green light to distribute the music throughout the fan base, writing, "I was able to contact some people and we came to the conclusion that because of DMB's loyal fan base following, honesty and patronage towards the band over the years, releasing these tracks should be, let's say, sort of a treat to the trading community . . . keep in touch and enjoy."

The songs hit Napster, and from there other people began hosting the tracks for download on personal websites. In his *Rolling Stone* article, Heller writes of the quickly spiraling effect on just one of those websites, hosted by a student at Perdue: "The day it went up—Monday, March 26th—it received 5,000 hits. By that Saturday, 40,000 folks had logged on. Their lines hopelessly jammed, Purdue shut the site down. Tang moved it elsewhere and 15,000 more Dave-heads got [*The Lillywhite Sessions*] before that site was also sealed off. Not that Tang's closures mattered. By then, the album was all over Napster, Gnutella, etc., and a feeding frenzy of downloading and burning began. The compare-and-contrast game between [*The Lillywhite Sessions*] and *Everyday* kicked into high gear on message boards. By modest estimates, 1,000,000 people have now heard at least part of [*The Lillywhite Sessions*]."

Although many fans were clearly happy to have the long-anticipated *Lillywhite Sessions* tracks, not everyone agreed on the ethics of its distribution. Some distribution sites encouraged fans to donate money to DMB's charity foundation, Bama Works, in "exchange" for the tracks, but not everyone agreed that such donations made up for taking the unreleased music. A column on nancies.org, "Babies and Lillywhites," sets forth the argument against downloading the tracks: "*The Lillywhite Sessions* (as they were creatively named) were originally supposed to be released. That's why they were recorded. We know that. Then they were shelved, for any number of reasons, supposed or real. Ultimately, the point is that they weren't supposed to be released. They were to be shelved, perhaps released a few years down the road, when Dave and Co. felt better about them. At that time, they didn't necessarily stand behind them. . . . *The Lillywhite Sessions* are everywhere; there's no way to 'get them back,' or to undo what's been done. I personally believe it's exemplary of the 'I'm supposed to get mine' mentality, where people are constantly denied in so many other ways in life that whenever they can get something in a backhanded fashion, they will, and they'll justify it. I'm not saying that everyone who has them is bad. I understand the rationale for wanting to have the *Sessions;* just don't sit there and try to justify people handing them out by saying that it's deserved, that as a fan you're *supposed* to have them. I don't buy into that at all."

Napster and independent websites weren't the only places leaking *The Lillywhite Sessions.* Once again, bootlegging reared its ugly head, with sellers on eBay and other online auction sites selling the CDs, sometimes under false pretenses. For example, a fan was offered the chance to purchase a pen on eBay for $20. Oh, and as a bonus, you got a burned CD of *The Lillywhite Sessions* thrown into the deal.

No matter what side of the debate fans fell on, at the end of the day there was no way to get *The Lillywhite Sessions* back. Not only were they part of the fan knowledge base at this point, but the leak was so big that it permeated the mass media. In the end, major media outlets joined fans in the sport of comparing *Everyday* and *The Lillywhite Sessions.* So widespread was *Lillywhite* distribution that even mainstream publications such as *Entertainment Weekly* published reviews of the album that wasn't. *Entertainment Weekly* for its part, incidentally, graded the album an A minus, dubbing it "the biggest phenomenon since Bob Dylan's *Basement Tapes*" and speculating that "If unauthorized downloads counted as sales, it probably would have gone gold, maybe even platinum, during its first couple of months on the free market known as Napster."

Regardless of what fans and critics had to say in praise of *The Lillywhite Sessions,* the fact remains that the band simply did not intend to have the music distributed in its current state. Not only did they not release the album, but it's clear from the songs' unmixed quality and Dave's sometimes clearly off-the-cuff, mumbled improvisations that *The Lillywhite Sessions* did not represent a finalized, polished product. In an April 17, 2002, interview with *Rolling Stone*, Matthews said, "When they first got out on the Web, it was like walking into a gallery and there's a crowd of people standing around looking at an unfinished painting and judging you for it. I can't blame the fans for wanting to hear the thing, but it can't fix the feeling that you've been robbed. There was an ugliness to it that left me feeling violated."

Not only did this period mark a pivotal point in DMB's history, it's also indicative of the climate of the music industry at the time. With the Internet's great strides, the powers that be struggled to deal with rapidly changing technology and the greater (and often illegal) accessibility and distribution of music, most notably through Napster. Truly, *The Lillywhite Sessions* was a product of the time and doubtless schooled many music industry insiders on the potential pitfalls of increasing digital accessibility.

With the *Everyday/Lillywhite Sessions* debacle still going strong, DMB commenced its summer tour in support of *Everyday* with a hometown show at UVA's Scott Stadium in Charlottesville on April 21, 2001—just a day after the ten-year anniversary of the full band's first public appearance at Charlottesville's Earth Day Festival. This marked DMB's first return to

Charlottesville since the *Crash* album debut at Trax in 1996. Despite the fact that several band members continued to live in Charlottesville and their allegiance to it had not waned, DMB had long since outgrown any of the venues that Charlottesville had to offer at the time. As a nod to its hometown crowd, advance tickets were offered to Charlottesville residents and UVA students.

The author of the Charlottesville local alternative paper *C-Ville*'s "DMBeat" column, Bill Ramsey, considers the Scott Stadium show to be a standout moment for locals who followed DMB. "My favorite memory is the 2001 homecoming concert at Scott Stadium at UVA. It had been years since the band had performed in town for lack of a large venue. Scott Stadium, the football field at UVA, had never hosted a concert before, so it was quite a unique event in several ways. [*C-Ville*] had a great time producing a special section that quickly became a popular item on eBay, and fans came from around the nation (if not the world, as I recall) for the show. [*C-Ville* editor in chief] Hawes [Spencer] hired a popular DMB cover band to play for the staff of *C-Ville* in the back of our offices. It was just a blast, one of those few moments when you feel musical magic in the air. On the evening of the show, Hawes and I boarded a hot-air balloon and flew over the stadium to photograph the crowd for the cover of a special two-disc CD the paper offered to fans to transfer the recording of the show. Of course, this was also the era of *Everyday,* viewed by many as a conscious attempt to make the band more radio friendly, but the show was very memorable, highlighted by the traditional sing-along to 'Ants Marching.'"

DMB fans know what they like. And they liked *The Lillywhite Sessions.* As the band continued along the road in support of the officially released *Everyday,* it was *The Lillywhite Sessions* songs fans were clamoring for. Thus the 2001 tour eventually morphed into a strange mixture of *Everyday* and *Lillywhite Sessions* tunes, with the unreleased songs now very much on display in a public forum.

Looking back, antsmarching.org cofounder Jake Vigliotti believes that this tour and the *Lillywhite* debacle marked a key turning point in the character of the DMB fan base. He explains, "I think that's the thing that really broke down the barrier between the fans and the band. Before *The Lillywhite Sessions,* there was always this sort of separation. So much information made it out from those sessions. Literally every day, information was coming out. And in a lot of ways it was really the fans that got that album out and made it complete. Because the fans just dominated. Here's the band, they come out and they're not happy with the album. They go out and make *Everyday* and now they're trying to push this album on people. They go to a show and the whole crowd is screaming for 'Big Eyed Fish' [from *The Lillywhite Sessions*], which hasn't even been released yet. The fans shouldn't even know about it. And, yet, they're screaming 'Big Eyed Fish! Big Eyed Fish!' So the band starts playing it for the rest of the tour.

"I'm not saying the band had to do that," he continues. "I'm not saying it's not good. But there's a fine line between who runs things, who decides things. And ultimately, it's the *band's* band—it's not the fans that get to pick out the songs. But at the same time, there's that sort of line between 'Okay, well, the fans don't want to hear "Angel" six shows in a row; they want to hear "Big Eyed Fish." I think that whole Lillywhite debacle is really what took the fans and sort of pushed them toward the front. Thankfully, now, I think things are less crazy than they were. I mean, fans still chant for songs, but I think things have calmed down a bit. But that time was just amazing."

For Stefan Lessard, it was somewhat difficult to see the fan antipathy toward *Everyday.* "I really wanted people to get behind *Everyday* because I had such a great experience making that record. When you have a great experience doing something, it's really hard to walk away from that. And, oh, everyone really loved the music we made when we wanted to kill one another and when we were in the darkest place and no one was having a good time. We'd spend all day outside because we hated the studio. *That* was *The Lillywhite Sessions.* Everyone was in cans, it wasn't even a real studio. Yet *those* are the songs everyone wants to hear. I went to L.A., I had an awesome time, I met new people, I worked in this great studio with a new engineer, and it was a whole new experience. And yet those songs the fans booed a lot at because they knew what they had just missed. After *Everyday* I was kind of bummed about the fact that people didn't like the songs."

Maybe *The Lillywhite Sessions* should never have been leaked. But the bottom line remains that it did. And for so many fans, official release or not, *The Lillywhite Sessions* is a vital and inextricable part of DMB's library of studio releases. When asked what he might do differently, knowing what he knows now, Lessard muses, "I typically don't look back and say I would change something. With the *Lillywhite* thing, it's interesting to look back on because that was six months of invested time that we put into those songs that people heard. They were unmixed, they were unfinished.

"Looking back," he continues, "if we had been smart, what I would have wanted to do is take what we had done in Haunted Hollow with Lillywhite and gone with Lillywhite to a completely new location—I would have taken us to Abbey Road or a studio in the Bahamas or to Hawaii. Someplace where the band felt like they could breathe again. Now, looking back on that, knowing what I know now, I might have suggested that we give Lillywhite one more try with the music that we'd already invested in. But let's go somewhere else—we can't finish that album at home. That's kind of what we did with *Big Whiskey* [2009]. We started writing in our studio in Virginia, we were there for a week writing and we got tons of jams, but then we needed to go somewhere else to really work on those jams and turn them into songs. I wouldn't have changed much, but I would have changed little things."

Despite all the hubbub about *The Lillywhite Sessions,* the tour soldiered on. Beginning on May 18, 2001, at the Pacific Bell Park show in San Francisco, California, Butch Taylor was officially brought into the lineup (where he would remain through the 2007 summer tour) to add keyboards and flesh out the *Everyday* sound.

It was during this 2001 tour that one of the most oft-cited favorite live moments happened on the first of DMB's three nights at Giants Stadium. On that night it seemed that the weather and DMB came together to create a spectacle. One fan, Jacqueline D'Angelo, who attended that June 11, 2001, show remembers, "The show was great all around. The seats, the songs, the company; the weather was the only thing working a little against us. It was cloudy and getting a little chilly as the show got on. We continued to sing, dance, and have a great time as we always did. We made it to the encore, and then we realized that the rain we were trying to escape was coming whether we liked it or not. The band played 'The Space Between' for song one of the encore. As they were finishing it up, we heard the thunder that was rumbling in the distance getting closer and closer. 'Two Step' started, and then more thunder. What happened next almost seemed like it was scripted or something. Dave started improvising lyrically about rain. We heard him say, 'Let it rain,' and as he did, the sky opened up and it poured buckets upon buckets of rain! Giants Stadium was filled with this magical energy that had the entire sixty-five-thousand-seat arena dancing, singing, and rejoicing in the rain. The fans were feeding off of the band, the rain, and the energy. The band was feeding off of the fans. It was *amazing.* You could see the looks on each band members' face. Carter, especially, was taking it all in. This rain went on until the completion of 'Two Step.' The strangest part was that it stopped raining when the song and the show were over. We all filed out of the stadium *soaking wet* and went back to our cars."

Matthew Khan was also there that night and agrees that it was magic. The Giants Stadium concert just happened to be his first, and he says it's that moment during "Two Step" that has kept him going to see DMB shows for the past ten years. Says Khan, "During the first verse of 'Two Step' Dave sings, 'Oh, darling, lay down . . . let it rain.' As Dave said the words 'Let it rain,' a lightning bolt screamed across the stadium opening and it started pouring rain. The crowd exploded in dance, and time literally slowed down. In my life, I've never experienced something so narcotic, and it is the reason that I follow this band around the country almost ten years later." (This version of "Two Step" was later released as a live track on *The Best of What's Around, Vol. 1.*)

In a 2009 video tribute to Giants Stadium shortly before its demolition to make way for the New Meadowlands Stadium, Dave Matthews recalled the evening: "I remember one time we played [Giants Stadium]. In the middle of our encore big clouds opened up and there was a massive hailstorm, pouring down on the stage. And people just lost their minds. There was such a good feeling in the place; it was like part of the show."

Unfortunately, the tone of the entire country was destined to change just a few months later on September 11, 2001. While this event clearly had larger implications on the entire country and the world in any number of ways, the music industry and DMB specifically felt the impact. Slated as the third *Everyday* single release on September 25, 2001, the song "When the World Ends" was held back due to its title. (In its place, "Everyday" was released, with a music video featuring Judah Friedlander of *30 Rock* fame wandering around Charlottesville and Manhattan hugging various characters, including NYC firefighters.) Additionally, "Crash into Me" was included on Clear Channel's list of 158 songs that were banned from the airwaves.

In many ways, 2001 was a strange year for DMB and its fan base, much as it was for America in general. With all of its peaks and valleys, though, the band ended 2001 with the fourth-highest-grossing tour of 2001 and the twenty-third-highest-grossing tour of all time in North America.

On the heels of the commotion that had surrounded *The Lillywhite Sessions* the year before, 2002 brought with it exactly what fans had been clamoring for: the official release of the *Lillywhite* songs—kind of. In January 2002 DMB's members returned to the studio to rerecord many of the songs they had worked on during the now-infamous Lillywhite Sessions in the form of *Busted Stuff.* Of the eleven songs included on the album, only two were new: "You Never Know" and "Where Are You Going." ("Where Are You Going" served as the lead single for *Busted Stuff* and was featured in the soundtrack of the 2002 movie *Mr. Deeds.* It received a Grammy nomination for Best Pop Performance by a Duo or Group in 2003 but lost to No Doubt's "Hey Baby.") The only catch was, Lillywhite himself wasn't actually involved with this resurrection of the songs.

For the recording of *Busted Stuff,* DMB returned to the Plant Studio, where they had recorded *Before These Crowded Streets.* Stephen Harris, who had served as the engineer on the original Lillywhite recordings, took over at the helm as producer. Notably, *Busted Stuff* is the only studio album to date that includes only the five founding members of DMB; no guest musicians were brought in for this recording.

Although *Busted Stuff* included many of the songs from *The Lillywhite Sessions,* they were reworked for the new album. As had been the case with earlier DMB albums, many of the songs had evolved and been refined over time based on the simple fact that they had been road tested over the course of the past years of touring. Although the foundations of the songs were generally the same, many of the lyrics changed and there was a levity that had not existed in the original *Lillywhite* versions. In an April 17, 2002, article with *Rolling Stone,* Dave explained the difference between *The Lillywhite Sessions* and *Busted Stuff:* "This time we felt that we were doing the songs justice. As they were, the sweetness of melancholy was missing, and they had a burdensome quality that was suffocating." *Entertainment Weekly* music critic Chris Willman agreed with Dave that the *Busted Stuff* versions were sweeter but questioned whether or not that was a good thing, writing "this is such a fascinatingly different take on (mostly) the same material that it almost whets your appetite for a third rendering. I'll own up to initially wishing the band hadn't gone back into the studio to fix what wasn't busted; it was that original Steve Lillywhite–produced set of recordings—with its uncharacteristically tense, terse, and compressed feel complementing Matthews' leap into murkier and more challenging depths as a writer—that converted me from skeptic to fan. His singing was surlier, too, when he was smack in the middle of his blue period, not two years and a life-affirming bout with fatherhood removed from the lyrics' more bitter sentiments. The new, self-produced sessions feel altogether sweeter, cleanly separating the players and goosing the still-eclectic signature sound. In particular, there's a good deal more of sax man LeRoi Moore, maybe to compensate for how lost he got in 2001's *Everyday* mix."

Busted Stuff ultimately received mixed reviews from fans and critics, likely due to a combination of factors. Some argue that the song versions included on the original *Lillywhite Sessions* leak were simply superior to those ultimately laid down for *Busted Stuff*. Also, for all the songs that *were* included on *Busted Stuff*, fan favorites (including "JTR" and "Sweet Up and Down") were not; however, interestingly, those songs continued to live on through live shows despite their omission from the later album. Finally, by the time *Busted Stuff* was released, the songs were no longer novel; most of the fan base had already been listening to them for years, so the excitement that generally accompanied album releases was somewhat watered down. But for the band, it was important to realize the songs fully and finish what they had started with Lillywhite. As Dave told *Rolling Stone*, "I feel like I've finished the picture. I'd left those songs in an ugly little pile. Going back was like seeing old friends again. This is some of the best stuff I've ever written and some of the best stuff the band has ever played." Ultimately, Stefan says, "It was fun to go in and re-do what we had done with Lillywhite. But I understand it wasn't the same. I still think there's some great songs on [*Busted Stuff*]."

After a nearly three-year buildup of anticipation for the songs included on *Busted Stuff*, the album was released on July 16, 2002. It went straight to number one on *Billboard*, giving DMB its second consecutive number one, and went on to be certified double platinum. While two million albums sold is certainly a significant number, it's interesting to note that *Everyday* outsold *Busted Stuff* by a million copies, particularly in light of all the media, discussion, and speculation that surrounded the songs.

DMB hit the live circuit hard in 2002 with a spring, summer, and winter tour. Although things contracted a little bit, with the band returning to amphitheaters rather than the stadiums of the most recent tours, DMB finished 2002 as the fifth-highest-grossing tour (and the sixteenth-highest-grossing tour of all time), being bested only by iconic acts such as Paul McCartney, the Rolling Stones, Cher, and the Billy Joel/Elton John double-bill tour. Notably, although DMB was not the highest-grossing act in 2002, it *was* the most popular in terms of ticket sales, playing to nearly as many people as Paul McCartney and the Rolling Stones combined played for that same year. As *Billboard* put it in its year-end tour wrap-up, "more people saw Dave Matthews Band this year than any other act on the planet, with some 1.4 million passing through the gates to the tune of $52.8 million, even with no stadiums on the route."

With such large audiences attending its shows (not to mention its own caravan of buses and big rigs crisscrossing the country), DMB began taking steps to ensure that their tours were as eco-friendly as possible. In 2002 it was announced that DMB would make an "unprecedented move in the entertainment industry" by certifying its 2002 national tour "Climate Cool." According to a press release of the time, DMB was "offsetting the carbon dioxide emissions produced during last year's tour in an effort to minimize the tour's impact on climate change. With its 2002 tour, the Dave

Matthews Band became the first musical group ever to receive this Climate Cool certification, joining organizations such as the 2002 Winter Olympic Games and leading Fortune 500 companies which have also received the nationally recognized certification mark." To accomplish this, the tour's emissions for 2002 were calculated; then the band offset them with the construction of wind turbines and tree-planting projects for a cumulative net-zero effect.

It was during the winter tour at the December 21, 2002, Madison Square Garden (MSG) stop in New York City that DMB put on yet another performance that has gone down as legendary. This particular night was rollicking from the very beginning, as evidenced by the midset "(All Along the) Watchtower" (usually reserved for the encore). The further into the set the band got, the more crazy the crowd became. Just when it seemed as though MSG couldn't be stirred up into any more of a fever pitch, it got even crazier. Mike Leone remembers, "From the moment DMB walked on-stage, the energy was insane. And on top of that, it was almost like some-one thought about the set list *too* much; it's perfectly scripted. It was the perfect storm: Christmastime in New York, holiday lights on Carter's drum set, and this amazing set list. They did 'Too Much' and started to go into this extended outro. Everyone was just sort of staring, and no one could figure out what was going on. Then, all of a sudden, James Brown comes onstage and does this microphone kick and is hooting and hollering. The band kicked into 'Sex Machine,' and the place just *erupted.* I mean, I've never heard an eruption like that at any show ever. Then James Brown and Dave start dancing side by side. And the thing is, that wasn't even the end of it. You've got cannons of confetti going off, then 'Halloween' and 'Ants Marching' to close. It just kept going and going like this volcano you were watching, waiting for it to erupt. Every so often I put that show on my iPod, and no matter where I am, the memory that comes back when I hear those confetti cannons go off is magic. Anyone who was there that night probably witnessed one of *the* best shows ever. It's hard to top." As the band played, MSG (which is built with the seating on a suspended "bowl" that allows the subway to run underneath the arena) literally began to rock. Bryan Narciso remembers the night as one of the highlights of the many shows he's seen since 1996. "I remember the crowd at MSG completely freaking out. Dave and James Brown were just getting down, and as it was happening, I had this feeling of pure joy at the excitement of it all."

In 2002 the popular fan site DMBML was shut down and antsmarching.org, founded by Jake Vigliotti and Matt Yette, stepped up to join nancies.org as the main cyber gathering spot for fans. Their plan was to build a new site that they thought would serve the huge audience DMBML had left in its wake. Combining Yette's technical skills and Vigliotti's extensive knowledge of the band (including detailed set lists that had previously been unavailable to the public), the two set out to create something "new and fresh." Clearly, their strategy worked. Yette remembers, "We had a thousand registered members the first day—we couldn't believe it." Antsmarching.org would become the most interactive site to date, allowing fans to track their own tour stats, including information such as how many shows they've been to, what songs they've seen, what guests they've seen, the rarity index of their show list, and more. (The rarity index of a given show or song is based on the frequency with which a song is played either in a given tour or over its lifetime. The higher the index, the rarer.) Information like this was becoming more and more valuable to fans as the years went by and people racked up huge numbers of shows. Fans continued to come, and by 2008 antsmarching.org was the most trafficked fan-based music website in the world.

In the years that have ensued since the *Lillywhite Sessions/Everyday/Busted Stuff* triad, *Everyday* songs have largely fallen by the wayside at live shows (with a few exceptions, including "When the World Ends" and "Everyday"). In fact, *Everyday* has the distinction of containing the one and only song DMB has ever recorded in-studio but never played a single time live: "Dreams of Our Fathers." Many of the songs originally recorded for *The Lillywhite Sessions,* on the other hand, have gone on to be concert staples ("Bartender" and "Grey Street") and remain in demand by fans. Despite the fact that the official versions of these songs were released on *Busted Stuff,* it seems as though fans most generally associate them with *The Lillywhite Sessions*. Although *The Lillywhite Sessions* was ultimately the album that wasn't, in the end it's inextricable from DMB's history (and in fact was a pivotal point for them) and their musical library.

Livin' the Dream

When trumpet player Ryan Svendsen was a freshman at UCLA in 2006, he set a goal for himself: to play onstage with his favorite group, Dave Matthews Band. Though he was only eighteen at the time, Ryan wasted no time setting about making his dream a reality. In 2006 he began contacting various DMB opening acts and management companies via MySpace in an effort to start working toward his goal. Before long, he got a hit: he received an e-mail from Robert Randolph and the Family Band, a Red Light Management artist and frequent opener for DMB. The message told him to come down to Los Angeles' House of Blues, where the band would be playing.

When the night arrived, Ryan showed up at House of Blues, trumpet in hand. With no idea what to do once he arrived, Ryan was looking for someone to speak with when he ran into Bruce Flohr of Red Light Management. Ryan explained his situation to Flohr, who had no idea what Ryan was talking about but nonetheless directed him to the greenroom. Once there, Ryan seized his opportunity and played a tune for Robert Randolph. Liking what he heard, Randolph invited Ryan to join the band onstage for the song "Diane" that night. Of the experience, Ryan says, "At one point, Robert just nodded to me to let me know it was my turn to solo, so I just went for it."

While the evening was an amazing experience for Ryan and a close hit, he still hadn't achieved his actual goal. Still determined to play with DMB, Ryan was thrilled when he heard that DMB would be casting musicians for the filming of the music video for "You & Me" in L.A. in 2009. Ryan realized this was his big chance. There was only one problem: to apply for the gig, participants had to have a SAG card, which he didn't. Still not deterred, Ryan e-mailed the casting director to plead his case.

Finally, the day before the "You & Me" shoot, the ever-hopeful Ryan began to gave up hope. That day, while driving from San Diego to Los

Angeles, his phone ran out of power. When he recharged the battery upon returning to L.A., he found both a voice mail and an e-mail from the "You & Me" casting director saying that Ryan was in for the video shoot but had to make contact as soon as possible. Ryan remembers, "I have no cell phone reception in my apartment whatsoever. So I ran out to the balcony, held my phone out to the side, and called him." The casting director delivered the bad news: "I wish you had called an hour ago." After giving yet another hard sell, Ryan waited on pins and needles for another thirty minutes until he finally heard that he was officially booked for "You & Me." The next day he would achieve his goal of playing with DMB. "I was overcome with joy," he remembers.

The day of the shoot, Ryan was the first extra to arrive on set. As he was waiting, in walked the whole band. Then it was time for work with a twelve-hour shoot that included ninety takes for a complex music video that included DMB playing "You & Me," backed by dozens of musicians. For Ryan, though, the hard work was worth it. "My dream came true," he says. "I got to play with DMB ninety times in one day. It was a huge mush of sound because the video was filmed in a hanger, but I knew that there I was, actually playing with DMB." As if this wasn't enough, during the lunch break, while all of the other extras left, Ryan had the opportunity to chat with all of the band members individually and even to receive musical advice from sax player Jeff Coffin.

Clearly Ryan made an impression on the band too. Nearly a year later, at the August 20, 2010, Chula Vista, California, show, upon seeing Ryan in the pit, fellow trumpet player Rashawn Ross handed Ryan his trumpet's Harmon mute, on which he had written "Keep playing." And, of course, Ryan will always have the "You & Me" video to relive the day his dream came true and he played with DMB. "I get to be part of this band's history forever, and that's pretty cool."

CHAPTER 6

SEARCHING FOR THE SOUND

TILL I GET TO THE END OF THIS TUNNEL

Whereas the Big Three years (1994–1998) had seen DMB on a steady studio-album release schedule with new albums coming every couple of years, in the wake of *Everyday/The Lillywhite Sessions*, new releases became far more sporadic. All at once, fans found themselves with much greater expanses of time between records than they were accustomed to. Interestingly, this was not necessarily mirrored onstage; throughout the period from 2003 to 2008, there were years when DMB debuted several new songs in a single tour. But what was happening onstage and what was happening in the studio were two very different things.

Though the decade opened with a focus on DMB's studio work, in 2003 the focus shifted back to the road and live shows. Despite the outcry that accompanied *Everyday*, fans remained avid in their dedication to and support of DMB, and business continued as usual. Although DMB went back to amphitheaters in lieu of stadiums as of 2003, the tour remained large, with many two-night stands at major venues throughout the United States. As opposed to the previous two years, which had featured a heavy rotation of *Lillywhite* and *Everyday* tunes, 2003 saw DMB return to its roots, with a solid rotation of songs from the Big Three albums back in the mix onstage. This tour did feature some strange quirks, however, with bizarre incidents such as eight fans making an unexpected trip to the hospital after being hit by lightening in the Alpine Valley Music Theatre (East Troy, Wisconsin) parking lots, and a hunting knife being thrown onstage between Dave Matthews and Boyd Tinsley during the Denver Pepsi Center stop in July.

Although stadiums were out for the 2003 tour, DMB played the largest single-night headlining show of its career at a dream venue on September 24, 2003, when they played before 121,282 people on Central Park's Great Lawn. The concert, the AOL Concert for Schools, was both sponsored by and simulcast live via America Online. Though the concert was free (assuming would-be attendees could get their hands on tickets, which was more difficult than one might imagine), ticket holders were encouraged to donate a minimum of $25 per ticket and proceeds were donated to the Fund for Public Schools of New York City and the Music Resource Center in Charlottesville, which provides music education for junior high and high school age students.

After waiting in line for hours to make a break for a good spot at the general admission Central Park show, fans ran the equivalent of three football fields once the gates opened in a bid to get to the front of the stage. One fan, Dave Tabachnik, remembers, "The rush that was felt upon the guards letting everyone run toward the stage in the open grass field was like nothing I ever experienced. I may never have run faster in my life." After an introduction by Mayor Michael Bloomberg, DMB came onstage to play a full set in the middle of Central Park, with New York City's skyline looming behind the stage. Bryan Narciso, who attended the concert, remembers that it was well worth the wait. "I've been to a hundred and four DMB shows, and I would probably rank that as a top-three show, for both the music and the entire experience. From a historical perspective, as a New Yorker, having my favorite band play that park was *mind-blowing*. I remember just looking back and seeing the skyline and then seeing the incomprehensibly massive crowd. From that perspective, I was blown away. It seemed to me that it was also hitting the band onstage that, Wow, we really are one of the biggest bands in the world. And even though they had been exactly that for so long, I think the massive nature of Central Park really drove it home for everyone, both onstage and off.

"From a musical standpoint," Narciso continues, "that show was awesome from start to finish. That raw energy the band had in the midnineties was definitely back at Central Park that night. Between Dave scatting, the interchanging lyrics for the 'Dancing Nancies' intro, and the 'New York, New York'/'Two Step' interpolation, it was the perfect musical experience. I just felt like DMB had some of their edge about them that night, where they just went off a little bit and let that music flow." On November 18, 2003, the historic concert was released on CD and DVD as *The Central Park Concert.*

The year 2003 was also the year that, for the first time since the genesis of DMB, band members stepped out to work on their own solo projects. In May 2003 Boyd released his first CD, *True Reflections.* In September of the same year, Dave released his own solo work, *Some Devil.* In support of his album, he toured with a separate group, Dave Matthews and Friends (which included, among others, Tim Reynolds and Phish's Trey Anastasio), during DMB's off-season in the winter of 2003–2004. Though these independent endeavors brought about a small level of anxiety among the fan base that solo projects might indicate some strife within the band, most took them with a grain of salt. Particularly since Dave had frequently played acoustic gigs with Tim Reynolds during the band's previous off-seasons, the idea of independent projects wasn't a completely novel one. And the band members themselves assured fans that their side projects wouldn't detract from their work together as DMB. In an October 2003 Q&A with Blender.com, Matthews said of *Some Devil*, "The drive was not so much to do something without the band as it was just to do something on my own. A lot of the record is just me and my guitar. It was just fun to go into a room and just make up some music and not think about anything but what was on my mind. The process is really different, but I think it's only going to make my love of working with the band even stronger." And according to Boyd, who later reflected on these solo projects in a 2005 interview with *Relix*, "I think that was a really great thing for us. Everyone was reaching out to different projects and just going into their own studios and working on different ideas. . . . Everything we learned from those individual projects, we brought to the table on [the album *Stand Up*]. I think it actually opened us up a lot musically working on those different projects."

While Dave and Boyd kept themselves occupied with music, Stefan decided to take on his own solo project, though not one of a musical variety. He explains, "Because I was so much younger than everyone else in the band and didn't go to college, there came a point when I realized our fans were sort of like my peers . . . a lot of them were around my age." It was with that in mind that Stefan launched his own website, IZStyle .com. (Though the idea for IZStyle.com was conceived in 2003, it did not actually launch until August 2004.) "I started the whole IZStyle website thinking it would be sort of a platform for me, instead of throwing a solo record out there. I didn't want that. I wanted something that sort of put me out there far away from everything else. So I started IZStyle.com thinking that I would form a community of like-minded people who were fans but who also would get into the other activities I like." With that concept in mind, IZStyle included a variety of content, with a focus on winter sports and the skating culture. Due to the emergence of MySpace around that same period, Stefan soon moved his primary discourse with fans over to the social networking site, for a time using MySpace as his primary mode of communicating directly with fans (though IZStyle.com is still up and running). Though he has changed his primary platform over time as the general populace has gravitated from one social networking site to another in conjunction with changing technological tides, it was through IZStyle and MySpace that Stefan began his avid online communication with the DMB fan base, discussing songs, shows, and completely unrelated topics on a regular basis.

Along with increased opportunities for social networking and motivating the fan base in myriad ways, the Web was changing music-sharing practices. As the 2000s rolled along, the open, permissive stance taken on digital issues by DMB and its management appeared increasingly smart and forward-thinking. As clearly evidenced by *The Lillywhite Sessions,* fans were able to share music online with increasing ease. More and more, the necessity for the old hard-copy tape and CD trading of yore was unnecessary. Though this certainly made the process of exchanging music much easier for fans, it took away a certain degree of the community-building element that earlier modes of trading had fostered. Mike Leone, who participated in B&P trading, explains the differences between old-school trading and the new digital age and easy accessibility that came along with it. "[In the old days] you would literally have to spend days researching, looking around for someone who had a show that you wanted. Then you had to spend days communicating back and forth—and remember, communication back then was not what it is today. It was e-mails through dial-up connections, and people didn't have BlackBerrys that they were checking every minute. Communication took the longest amount of time. Then there was the deal making. It literally was a process. And at the end of the process it was kind of like completing a big project at work: you have a goal and timelines and estimates—that's really what trading tapes was like. When you actually received the tapes after all this communication, then the tape dubbing, packaging, and snail mailing the cassettes, it was a job well done. On top of that, there was the thrill of knowing you were one of a small group of a people that had that show on tape. You had something that was valuable—not in a dollar amount, but to you. It was challenging, and, more than that, it was a full-blown hobby. It wasn't like it is now. I think that the older generation of fans alone can really appreciate the effort that went into it. There had to be a lot of passion behind it because it involved a huge amount of work."

In 2003, DMB updated its taping policy to state, "posting audio or video files on web sites for streaming to or downloading by the public, is not authorized." This update, according to DMB's site, was made in an effort to maintain the original intent of the taping policy, which had the following underlying goal in mind: "In addition to helping fans re-create the live experience, we hope tape trading will foster greater interaction within the fan community. Any method of trading that does not involve personal fan interaction defeats the spirit of this goal of the taping policy and is not authorized."

Bill Lakenan remembers, "I found it really interesting to watch DMB management's reaction from afar. Because at first they were staunchly opposed to DMB being shared online. They *really* liked the community that developed around tape trading. They really fostered that and thought that, in the end, it benefited them by reinforcing and strengthening their fan base. But when it came to sharing music online, they were against it. In a statement at the time, they said they were all for taping and trading as a means of building their community but didn't think that nameless, faceless FTP servers did much to build relationships within the fan base."

Though management ultimately allowed taping and trading to continue, they were right in feeling that free-for-all downloading would change things. Though the high traffic of fan-based website message boards such as antsmarching.org clearly prove that fans still have plenty of things to discuss, for the most part these discussions have moved away from trading and one-on-one music-sharing. Says Jake Vigliotti, "That's one thing we've struggled with at antsmarching.org. We've tried our best to make it interactive because you have to sign up and you have to do it through a message board. We're trying to keep that old style of communication going. But it's difficult now, it's really difficult." Nate Vandemark agrees that the scene has changed with the emergence of digital downloads: "One of the big things that kept me so attracted to DMB from 1996 to 2002 was the fact that I was constantly meeting new people. Which I still do, but now it's not because of tape trading. I meet people for, like, an afternoon at a show—it's not an actual friendship the majority of the time. Whereas, with trading, you were in constant correspondence, going back and forth for years at a time getting shows."

Indeed, digital accessibility changed taping and trading in the most marked fashion yet. During the 2000s, sites such as DreamingTree.org and etree.org emerged, which allowed tapers to directly upload digital recordings of shows for free-for-all download distribution. Rather than orchestrating a trade, community members now only had to go to these sites, click a few buttons, and download shows directly to their computer. Of all the changes that occurred in the taping and trading community over the course of the past decade, this one marked the biggest transition. No longer was it necessary for fans to come together, to communicate via e-mails or message boards or in person to exchange one show for another. No longer was it necessary to wait for weeks (if not months) after a show to even have a hope of obtaining a recording. Suddenly everything was instantaneous and available with just the click of a mouse. The once studiously adhered to two-week rule, still technically in effect, became somewhat of a joke as more and more tapers got their shows up to the sites within twenty-four hours—and sometimes the actual night of the show.

Even on the often rogue Internet, DMB fans have for the most part remained an orderly, self-policing bunch. Strict rules govern the way music can be distributed: it must be lossless to preserve its integrity. That means MP3 files cannot be disseminated; only the lossless FLAC and SHN formats will cut it. And despite the abundance of shows available and the ease of distributing and obtaining them, no recording may be uploaded to hot-spot sites such as DreamingTree.org until the show has actually been verified. This isn't an issue with recent shows, where set lists are abundantly available (the DMB crew updates its site with real-time set lists, and any other number of fan sites and mobile applications do the same), but the verification rules *do* come into play when it comes to electronically spreading older shows for which information is not as readily available.

Solo projects and technological debates aside, once the summer of 2004 rolled around, the band was once again on the road together. With the most recent studio album, *Busted Stuff,* now two years behind them, fans started to look forward to the next official DMB release. It was known that DMB had spent some time in the recording studio prior to the summer tour, and, based on the 2004 song debuts, things looked good. Throughout the course of the summer, DMB regularly included a handful of new songs in their sets, including "Good, Good Time," "Sugar Will," "Crazy-Easy," "Hello Again," and "Joy Ride." Though somewhat rough, with changeable lyrics, these new songs were quite well received and seemed to bode very well for the next album. It appeared that fans could rest assured that the pre-*Everyday* DMB was back, with acoustically driven, sweeping songs that incorporated the entire band. Nate Vandemark remembers, "I think everyone was just waiting for DMB to go back to their roots, which is exactly what seemed to be happening with 2004 tour songs like 'Crazy-Easy,'

'Hello Again,' and 'Joy Ride.' Those new songs in 2004 had the same vibe the band had in 1996: they were exciting, they were old-school-sounding songs, and they were just *good*. It was Dave on acoustic instead of baritone. It was exciting to hear those songs. I would say at that point I thought that was the direction the band was going. That they'd record those 2004 tour songs and that's what would eventually turn up on their next studio album."

The 2004 tour also saw DMB play another large-scale free show, somewhat reminiscent of the previous year's Central Park gig. This time, though, DMB switched coasts, hosting a free benefit concert at San Francisco's Golden Gate Park on September 12, 2004. (The show was released as the second album in the *Live Trax* series in December 2004.) A million dollars in proceeds from this gig went to benefit local charities working for a variety of causes including area parks, music education, and AIDS research; in recognition of this, San Francisco Mayor Gavin Newsom announced that September 12, 2004, was officially Dave Matthews Band Day. In a press release about the event, Mayor Newsom said, "Dave Matthews Band's generosity stands out as a model of private/public partnership."

Once again, fans waited for hours to make the run across the field to the stage. One fan, Loren Byrne, remembers, "My best college buddy and I decided to fly from the East Coast to San Francisco to attend the Golden Gate Park show. Since the show was general admission, we wanted to be able to get the best seats possible. We showed up at the park at five A.M. for the midafternoon show. It was chilly and foggy, but about a hundred people were already in line and having a good time. We chatted with those around us to pass the time, which went by fast. As the time to enter the gates approached, anticipation was high and we began plotting our strategy to get as close to the stage as possible: run faster than we ever had before! The gates were about two football fields away from the stage, but we ran as fast as we could the entire way. We ended up in the second row, center stage."

Once inside, Byrne and other patient fans were rewarded with a guest spot by Carlos Santana, who played with DMB on "Sugar Will," "All Along the Watchtower," and "Stay (Wasting Time)." Watching Santana play on stage with DMB, one fan, Mike Rofe, remembers, was amazing. "I remember [Santana] really waiting the song out before he jumped in. I was amazed at how disciplined he was as a guitarist, to not just dive in, but to really wait for the right moment." Also according to Rofe, the Golden Gate Park show included the perfect combination of elements that make for the best DMB shows. "Being in San Francisco on a big grass field dancing and listening to DMB was a magical combo for me. It felt like the whole crowd was on the same page and the mood was just right. Another aspect of any great show is how in tune the band and crowd are. People talk about Bruce Springsteen concerts being a religious experience; I think if you really want to feel the religion of DMB, the whole mood has to be right. The venue and the crowd is a huge part of that. The show at Golden Gate Park was the first time I really felt that with DMB."

In addition to its own headline tour, DMB also lent its support to the 2004 Vote for Change tour. In this series of Midwest and East Coast shows, DMB played with a variety of other acts including Bruce Springsteen, Neil Young, Bonnie Raitt, and Ben Harper & the Innocent Criminals, encouraging audience members to get out and vote in the 2004 George W. Bush versus John Kerry election.

At the end of the 2004 tour, Red Light Management announced that it would be releasing a new series of live recordings, *Live Trax*, beginning with the December 8, 1998, Worcester's Centrum Centre (Worcester, Massachusetts) show. According to Pete Paszkowski, who attended the show, it was the perfect inaugural choice for this series. "Those winter arena shows tend to get crazy, but this one was particularly out of control. I'll never forget that version of 'The Last Stop.' As they were playing it, I just kept thinking, 'Please don't stop, please don't stop.' And they didn't. For almost twenty minutes, there was a stage full of musicians, with Béla Fleck, Timmy [Reynolds], and DMB just all playing their hearts out as the crowd was going insane." Unlike DMB's previously released live recordings (with a few exceptions that would come later on, with the 2006 Boston, Massachusetts, Fenway Park *Live Trax, Vol. 6* leading the pack), the *Live Trax* series was distributed directly through DMB's website, in conjunction with Musictoday. The *Live Trax* series was available for order in CD format and also, for the first time, in both MP3 and FLAC digital download format. Though many of the *Live Trax* show recordings were already available through taping and trading, fans were nonetheless enthusiastic about the series, which provided crisp, clean alternatives to recordings that had either never been high quality in the first place due to the inferiority of earlier taping technology or had lost quality through generations of trading.

As for studio recordings, in early 2005, it was announced that producer Mark Batson would head up DMB's next studio album, slated for release that summer. The choice was a bit surprising, as Batson was best known for producing rap and R&B acts, such as Dr. Dre, Jay-Z, and Eminem. However, Batson represented a conscious decision on the part of the band, which wanted to experiment a bit with different types of production. DMB returned once again to Haunted Hollow (finished and much improved since the fateful *Lillywhite Sessions*) and began recording with Batson in January 2005. Batson incorporated all of the band members into the songwriting process by having each member play various licks and building songs around them.

Nate Vandemark remembers being pleased when he heard about the recording process. "I remember there was this one interview with Carter when he was talking about how great the experience of recording the album was because they were recording in an old-school fashion with all of them in one room together." They were also clearly experimenting instrumentally, with various band members playing instruments that were not their standard fare: Stefan (bass), for example, picked up a guitar; Boyd (violin) plucked away on a mandolin; and Dave (guitar) played some piano. From there, DMB recorded with guest musicians (including Batson) on keys and percussion. Also notable about *Stand Up* are the often political lyrics, as clearly evidenced on the album's first single, "American Baby." As had been the case with *The Lillywhite Sessions,* fans were privy to information from the recording studio; however, it was distributed in a very organized fashion through a website the band set up specifically for *Stand Up,* where fans could hear clips and watch videos.

Prior to the album's official release on May 10, 2005, VH1.com streamed *Stand Up* in its entirety. To celebrate, DMB played a special release show at New York's Roseland Ballroom on May 9, which was broadcast live on AOL. Simultaneously released as a physical CD and (for the first time) digitally via iTunes, *Stand Up* gave DMB its fourth consecutive number one debut and went platinum before two months had passed. (Though *Stand Up* was available on iTunes upon release, it wasn't until April 2006 that DMB's back catalog of studio albums was released through the digital outlet.)

Fans were, once again, confused. Although *Stand Up* was not met with the same level of dismay and outcry *Everyday* had been, it was still unexpected and, for some, somewhat unsatisfying. Nate Vandemark says that although he liked *Stand Up* at the time it was released, it certainly wasn't what he was expecting to hear. "I was anticipating that the next time DMB went into the studio, they would hear what the fans were saying and go back to their roots, so to speak, releasing something that was more in tune with the Big Three and the early stuff. It was just kind of frustrating waiting for that to happen. The anticipation was running high." Of all the beloved song debuts from the summer before and the initial Charlottesville recordings in 2004, only one of them ("Hello Again") made the final cut. The songs included on *Stand Up* were highly produced and, once again, not in line with the quintessential DMB sound. Yet again, the violin and horns seemed to fade into the background. In *Rolling Stone*'s review of *Stand Up*, Christian Hoard wrote, "Where 2001's manicured *Everyday* turned DMB into a world-beating, chart-busting juggernaut, *Stand Up* is the sound of a veteran outfit navigating between jammy mojo and pop-wise charm. More than most bands, DMB needs a skilled producer to edit out the fatty jam sessions . . . the result is a disc whose unfussy demeanor conceals a mountain of overdubs and deftly edited jams."

Of *Stand Up*, Stefan says, "We've never recorded 'Crazy-Easy,' we've never recorded 'Joyride,' we did 'Hello Again' for *Stand Up*, and a lot of people think it's the best song on the album. I agree in a sense because it's the band—*Stand Up* was a really different record for us because there was a lot of rubbing against the grain. It was fun in a lot of ways, but I had moments there where I'd walk in and I'm like, 'I'm pretty sure that's not my bass. It's too clean-sounding, too hip-hop-sounding. I'm pretty sure I didn't play on this song.' Yet that's what was put on the record. It sort of felt like it was out of my hands. People dogged me for a while about the guitar stuff on 'Hunger for the Great Light,' but it's funny because the way it was recorded is not the way I had written it. The way it was recorded is because that's how Batson recorded it and the way it was mixed and everything that came after."

In a June 16, 2005, article in *Rolling Stone*, Mark Batson explained, "Some people perceive [DMB] on record to be smooth, and since I make records that bump and bang, the band felt I might be able to help them capture their vibe. But they also wanted to begin a new era with a new sound. So *Stand Up*, in a funny kind of way, was like approaching a first album—like an introduction to the twenty-first-century Dave Matthews Band." The problem, it seemed, was that fans preferred the twentieth-century version of DMB—at least in the studio.

Although fans weren't necessarily as excited about the new studio songs that were played during the 2005 *Stand Up* promotional tour as they had been about debuts in the past, as always DMB mixed it up onstage, playing a variety of tunes from its whole career. Fans' primary complaints about *Stand Up* songs were that they weren't evolving or giving the band room to explore onstage, which is where DMB has historically always shone live. And indeed, with the exception of "You Might Die Trying" and, to a lesser extent, "American Baby Intro," as had been the case with many of the *Everyday* songs before, many of the *Stand Up* songs did not go through much of an evolution onstage and, as the years have passed, have proved themselves less durable live than some of DMB's earlier work.

For many fans, a divide between what they expected of DMB in the studio versus what was expected onstage began to emerge. The band was still creating new songs and jamming to old ones out on the road, and the new songs developed live were for the most part very well received. But for some reason, since 2001 many of the new "road-tested" songs hadn't been making it through the recording cut. Nate Vandemark remembers that, though some fans may not have been completely pleased with DMB's studio works, the live shows were a different story. "I can't think of a year where the live shows were ever suffering at all. They were good . . . they were DMB shows."

Indeed, there were great moments in the midst of the 2005 tour. Beginning on September 9, 2005, DMB played a four-night stand at Red Rocks (which would go on to wide release in both CD and DVD format as *Weekend on the Rocks*), which most fans and critics agreed was nothing short of mind-bending. Originally scheduled as a three-night stand, an additional night was tacked on to the end as a benefit show, with all proceeds going to aid the victims of Hurricane Katrina. One fan, Alan Gonzalez, who attended all four nights at Red Rocks, remembers the long weekend as one of his most memorable DMB experiences to date. "It was maybe the best weekend of my life. Spending four days watching my favorite band, hanging with hard-core fans from all over the map—East Coast, West Coast, everywhere—it was unbelievable. That venue, the way the stage is, the band is just right there with you. It's seventy very steep rows, so you're very, very close no matter where you sit. Not to mention, the acoustics in the venue are unbelievable. The Denver city lights were right behind the stage and visible from about thirty rows up, and the fire dancer was reflected off the rocks." (The fire dancer has been a DMB mascot of sorts since the 1990s. Dave drew this somewhat obscure figure in answer to the question, "What does the crowd look like to you from onstage?" The fire dancer has been a familiar image on fan memorabilia for years and was also the cover image for *Stand Up*.)

According to Gonzalez, the highlight of the four-day extravaganza occurred during the encore of the September 11 show. "The whole show that night was phenomenal: Stefan played a 'Star-Spangled Banner' intro into 'Watchtower,' and Boyd had the best solo I've ever heard him play in 'Lie in Our Graves.' After 'Granny,' everyone started chanting, 'Halloween'! 'Halloween'! Then you could see the band chatting onstage, and I was like, No, there's no way they're going to play it. There's no way. People started yelling as loud as they could. Then you could hear the band sort of warming up—and it was 'Halloween'! Oh my God, I've never seen an explosion like that ever before in my life—it was like an eruption, like a volcano. That was the single most amazing moment I've ever witnessed in my life. 'Halloween' wasn't on the set list, DMB just added it because everyone was going crazy. Then, when it was over, everyone started chanting, 'Thank you, Dave! Thank you, Dave!' I've never seen people chant that before. You could tell the band thought it was cool."

Aside from its own shows, DMB was becoming increasingly visible at concerts designed to raise public awareness about environmental and political issues, of which there were many during George W. Bush's administration in the turbulent years that followed 9/11. On July 2, 2005, DMB joined a host of other musicians as part of the ten simultaneous Live 8 concerts worldwide designed to bring attention to G8 Summit issues. The U.S. concert was held at the Philadelphia Museum of Art, with more than one million attendees present (the concert was also widely broadcast on television). Live 8 happened to occur in the midst of DMB's two-night stand at SPAC in Saratoga Springs, New York, which required the band to play two shows on July 2—one in Philadelphia and one later that night at SPAC. DMB's road crew shared their experience on the Road page of the band's official website, writing, "What an incredible experience we all had today. We got an early start on site for the Live 8 show. It was amazing how many people were already there when we arrived at 6:30 A.M. It was quite a scene back stage as the eclectic mix of bands prepared for their turn to play. DMB rocked 4 strong songs for their set, which was said to have been watched by millions worldwide. Immediately following the set in Philly, we rushed to the airport for a quick flight back to Saratoga Springs and arrived with about an hour and a half to go before set time. Just enough time to gather our thoughts before putting on another show. Admittedly, we were all a bit tired after the whirlwind we had just been through, but that changed immediately when DMB hit the stage to the roar of the eagerly awaiting audience. The band members were so moved by the energy of the crowd tonight that they took a moment between songs to thank and applaud the audience for their exuberance."

Though DMB ended 2005 as the ninth-highest-grossing act of the year, it was in second place for most tickets sold, with a total of 1.21 million fans in attendance during the year. (This disparity between gross revenue and tickets sold is in large part due to DMB's lower-than-average ticket prices, with DMB's average ticket at $47.09.) By the end of 2005, it was the only act to finish in the top ten highest-grossing list five times over the course of the past ten years.

Less than three months after *Stand Up*'s May 2005 release, talk of DMB's next studio album was already beginning, with Dave telling *Rolling Stone* that DMB planned to reconvene with Mark Batson prior to the 2006 tour kickoff. Through his IZStyle website, Stefan invited fans into the studio with the band for the first time in spring 2006, blogging about how the whole process worked on his Haunted Hollow Diaries page. Though he didn't specifically mention what songs were being worked on, Stefan illuminated the entire process, explaining everything from how jam sessions went down to how songs were built to what dinnertime at Haunted Hollow was like.

As had happened so many times in the past during non-album-promotion years, in summer 2006, new tunes hit the circuit. This year they were "Break Free," "Idea of You," "Can't Stop," "Kill the King," "Sister," and fan favorite "Shotgun." Once again, fans kept their fingers crossed that those songs would go on to make it onto the new studio album, despite the fact that they were somewhat wary of Batson, based on his previous work with *Stand Up.* Presumably, however, it was fair to assume that these new tour songs did have a legitimate shot at making an album cut. On his Haunted Hollow Diaries blog, Stefan wrote, "Our producer realizes that a lot of the words and melodies will be discovered during the tour this summer, so for now he just wants to set up a foundation for us to work with."

The 2006 summer tour saw DMB's onstage lineup expand once again, with the addition of trumpeter Rashawn Ross (Soulive, Yerba Buena), who had played a handful of shows with DMB in 2005. Discovered by LeRoi Moore, Rashawn was brought in to create a horn section. Interestingly, though the horns on DMB's most recent studio work were not as prominent as they had once been, onstage the horns were more pronounced than ever, thanks to the collaborative work of LeRoi and Rashawn.

Following a few months of extensive rumors, DMB booked a two-night stand at Boston's Fenway Park. The then-ninety-four-year-old ballpark was a highly selective venue; in 2003 Bruce Springsteen had played Fenway's first concert since 1973, and in the years that followed, only one act per year was allowed to play the park. In 2006 that act was DMB. One fan, Graham Johnson, who attended the two-night stand, particularly remembers "Grace Is Gone" (played on night two) as a standout performance. Says Johnson, "I had never heard the extended hoedown outro to 'Grace Is Gone' live before. It started so subtly and just kept building. It was as if DMB had me in a trance with it. I literally just stood there with a big grin on my face and was so swept up in the moment." In a nod to the tradition-steeped ballpark, on night two DMB played a cover of Neil Diamond's "Sweet Caroline" (a song that rowdy Fenway crowds traditionally sing before the bottom of the eighth inning at Red Sox games) in the eighth-song slot. The ballpark went crazy as two of the Fenway Faithfuls' favorite worlds collided: DMB and baseball. The evenings were also filled with boisterous pickup chants of "Yankees suck" ringing throughout the stadium, making it impossible to forget for a moment that DMB was in Red Sox territory. The four-disc recording of this show, *Live Trax, Vol. 6,* marked the first edition of the series available in stores, rather than just direct from the DMB website. This disc was opened up to wide release in large part because of retailers' demand in the Boston area.

The 2006 tour ended with a hometown stand in Charlottesville. Once again, a large length of time had passed between DMB's Charlottesville appearances—the band's last show there had been the Scott Stadium concert in 2001. This time around, DMB appropriately played the grand opening of UVA's new John Paul Jones Arena. In attendance that night, Kim Zaepfel remembers, "With it being the first time the band played their hometown in five years, expectations were incredibly high. The air pulsated with electricity." All was well until the encore of the show when, at the end of "American Baby Intro," a man dressed in a trench coat appeared menacingly onstage. Carter Beauford looked over and spotted the intruder (who has, appropriately, been dubbed Trench Coat Man in DMB circles), and chucked a drumstick at him. DMB security tackled him, and the show continued—but not as it was supposed to. Though DMB had planned to play "The Last Stop" as the final song of the night following "American Baby Intro" according to the set list, the fan favorite and much-coveted song was abandoned and DMB substituted the far more frequently played "Stay (Wasting Time)." In the years that followed, the Trench Coat Man has become notorious for robbing fans of "The Last Stop" that night, which did not appear again until almost four years later at the July 31, 2010, West Palm Beach show, despite fans' frequent chanted pleas.

In early 2007 DMB went back to Haunted Hollow with Mark Batson, recording at least partial versions of many of the songs that had debuted during the 2006 tour, including "Shotgun," "Idea of You," and "Break Free." "Sweet Up and Down," which had appeared on The Lillywhite Sessions but hadn't made the Busted Stuff cut, was also readdressed during those recording sessions. Unbeknown to fans at the time, this would be DMB's final recording session with Batson.

Throughout 2007, little bits of news floated around about DMB's new album, on message boards, in the mass media, and from various band members. In March 2007 Billboard wrote that a new DMB album could be expected just a few months later, in July. That didn't happen and things became nebulous. Recording sessions were vaguely mentioned by band members and a studio album was on fans' minds, but solid information wasn't really coming.

By 2007, much of the mainstream buzz that had swirled around DMB from the days of Under the Table through the Everyday/Lillywhite period had died down. Not only had the band's most recent release, Stand Up, already been on the shelves for two years, but it had received a far mellower mass media/pop culture reception than its previous studio efforts. Furthermore, the music tide had changed, with mainstream tastes favoring the tighter rock sound of groups such as the White Stripes, the Strokes, and the Killers. Though DMB's tours continued to rank in the top-ten-grossing acts on an annual basis, its audiences contracted a bit. Since fewer albums were coming out to promote (and thus the band had less media exposure and radio airtime), the scene stabilized somewhat, with fewer people attending shows simply based on the credit of a recent single or buzz among their friends. Without the rush of new people coming in the door that previous years had seen, the DMB showgoing crowd once again consisted primarily of die-hard fans. Even so, there were enough diehards out there to fill 20,000-plus-capacity amphitheaters for two nights in a row.

Though DMB was not a complete stranger to international audiences, its attention had historically been primarily on domestic venues. In 2007, what would become a more consistent focus on international touring began, with the full band playing a handful of Australian and European tour dates in the spring. Portugal's Clube de Fãs [Fan Club] DMB cofounder Inês Ventura explains that the concert scene in Portugal is different from that in America, primarily because the infrequency of shows means that fans "focus more on the music and on band-crowd interaction, while Americans focus more on the experience of a show as a whole." Despite the fact that DMB's May 25, 2007, Pavilhão Atlântico (Lisbon, Portugal) show (later officially released as *Live Trax, Vol. 10*) was the first time the band had played on Portuguese soil, Ventura remembers that 20,000 well-versed fans came out of the woodwork. "There wasn't any visible significant fan movement prior to the Lisbon show. The show was barely advertised, and yet the venue was packed with people who seemed to be too much into what was going on onstage to be just random curious concertgoers. There was a lot of screaming, smiling, even tears of joy. The moment the band played the first chords of 'Everyday,' the crowd just exploded into 'Honey, honey' chants. It seemed as though all of that long-term desire to see the band turned into this massive energy of sound. And when Dave stepped up to the microphone after 'Gravedigger' and said, 'I gotta tell y'all, this is the livest audience we've ever seen,' there's no way of describing the roar in the venue. It was a giant communion—almost like a collective high." DMB, it would seem, felt the high as well. When the band returned to Portugal for the Optimus Alive show on July 11, 2009, Dave told a reporter with Portugal's *Top+*, "The last time we were here, that was the greatest audience we've ever been in front of. It was a little bit scary, almost, because the energy was *awesome*."

With new European experiences under their belt, DMB turned their attention back to its well-worn American summer touring path, though the 2007 summer tour started much later than usual, on August 1 in Mansfield, Massachusetts (as opposed to the band's usual late-May start). Again, new songs emerged, including "Eh Hee" (which Dave released as a solo work via iTunes), "A Dream So Real," "#27," and "Cornbread."

On September 6, DMB headlined a special concert for Virginia Tech in response to the horrific on-campus shootings the spring before. Also on the bill that evening were John Mayer, Nas, and Phil Vassar, all of whom played the show for free. Free tickets were provided for Virginia Tech students and faculty, and additional tickets were available for public sale. In attendance that evening, Kim Zaepfel remembers the evening as an extremely special one. "As the Hokies geared up for DMB, the chants of 'We are VT' and 'Hokie, Hokie High' bounced around the stadium almost as though it were an audible stadium wave. For a minute the crowd almost convinced me that I (an avid anti-Hokie) was a Virginia Tech supporter. Almost. But it was hard not to absorb the feeling of unity and solidarity. The chants continued throughout the entire show during song breaks. I still get goose bumps thinking about it: proud, resilient, healing Virginia Tech. The band wasn't there for money (there was no charge for student tickets), they weren't there for glory (a good portion of the audience were not DMB fans), they were there to be a catalyst in the healing process. Dave told us all about the little red van and the 'little holes' they used to play in Blacksburg, Virginia. Then David Ryan Harris shows up on stage, and they impromptu morph 'Jimi Thing' into Bob Marley's 'Three Little Birds': 'Don't worry bout a thing . . . 'cause every little thing is gonna be all right.' Over and over and over again. I don't know if Dave didn't remember the rest of the words (he did sing the first verse) or if it was the poignancy of the lyric, but it became a chant, a mantra, something for all of us to hang on to. As the students went back to the dorms and the rest of us on to our vehicles, we heard tinkles of laughter and saw nothing but smiles and hand holding everywhere. It was like we were all of a sudden family, and we'd come through something horrible just to experience this intense and overwhelming sense of love and community. There was nothing but love that night, and no one was an outsider. We were welcomed into the fold, and we became a part of this thing, this moment, this amazing evening that I will never forget. It wasn't about the set list. Hell, it wasn't even necessarily about the Dave Matthews Band. It was about the Hokies, about love, unity, and the ability to smile and remember that everything was gonna be all right."

Indeed, throughout the years, it's been moments like these when DMB and the joy their music has to offer really shine through at their brightest. In a 2009 *Relix* interview, Matthews said, "There's no real point in mourning all the sadness and suffering in the world. . . . So this is my therapy, to sing about the end of the world and dance. We don't find solutions in despair—we find solutions in the defiance of it. All we have to do is turn the TV on or open the newspaper to see how much disaster and horror there is. Everybody needs a little *horn section.*"

Though the 2007 U.S. tour was a short one, it ended with a bang at the Hollywood Bowl. On the final night of both the two-night stand and the tour, DMB brought a number of guests onstage throughout the evening, including Charlottesville musician Danny Barnes, DMB crew member and guitarist Joe Lawlor, John Mayer, and Stephen and Ziggy Marley. Pete Paszkowski, who traveled cross-country from Massachusetts to attend the show that evening, remembers that the night full of surprises made the long trip well worth it. "I just could *not* believe the show that unfolded: 'Shotgun,' 'Exodus,' '#34.' 'Exodus' was crazy with the Marley brothers. They have about ten people in their band, including the flag guy, who just has this flag and waves it around onstage. So when DMB played 'Exodus,' they brought the Marleys and their entire band out—there're about, like, fifteen people onstage at once. It was the craziest thing. Then, of course, '#34' (which is usually instrumental only and rare at that) was played with lyrics for the first time since 1993 in honor of Dave's wife's thirty-fourth birthday. '#34' with words is one of those holy grails to see live. It felt so special. All I could think was how lucky I was to be there at that moment. DMB also invited their entire crew onstage at the end of the show in honor of the tour's end. Everyone was just up there, clapping and taking pictures. That was a great moment to witness—seeing them say good-bye and thank you. Truly a stellar show."

Shortly after the 2007 tour ended, DMB went back to Haunted Hollow to work on an eclectic variety of songs that included new jams, as well as songs that had appeared on the 2006 and 2007 tours. In winter 2008, the band moved production to Studio Litho in Seattle, where it continued working on a large selection of songs, many of which would go on to make the cut on DMB's next studio album. With the announcement of summer tour dates in March 2008 came additional welcome news for fans: a new producer had finally been selected for the much-delayed studio album. DMB was bringing in Rob Cavallo (who had previously worked with Green Day, My Chemical Romance, and Alanis Morissette). For fans, this seemed like a more natural choice than some of the band's more recent producers and served to heighten excitement about the now much-delayed next album.

When DMB emerged onstage in the summer of 2008, it sounded much different. After nearly ten years, keyboardist Butch Taylor had abruptly left the band prior to the commencement of the tour. Tim Reynolds, much beloved by fans, stepped in for a full DMB tour for the first time since fall 1998. Many of the keyboard fills that had been present in recent years were now replaced with electric guitar riffs, making for a much louder and rocked-out DMB than fans had seen in quite some time.

Nate Vandemark remembers that the 2008 tour started off with a bang. "Everyone was excited because Tim Reynolds was back with the band and we had stellar set lists, the likes of which we hadn't seen in years." Indeed, from the time the 2008 tour opened on May 30, 2008, at the Post Gazette Pavilion in Burgettstown, Pennsylvania, to the June 28 show at the Nissan Pavilion in Bristow, Virginia, it seemed as though everything was not only back on track but better than ever.

No one could have known that in the blink of an eye, *everything* was about to change.

Superfan

If you've come in contact with a caped crusader at a show before, chances are you've met Pete Paszkowski. A fan since 1996, Pete happened upon his concertgoing alter ego by accident. It was at the August 28, 2004, Carson, California, Home Depot Center when, Pete explains, "A girl gave this red cape to me because it was the show right after my birthday. She said I was going to be the King of the Home Depot Center that evening."

Pete wasn't the only one in costume that night. "One of my friends wore a court jester hat, and we had a blast up there in the second row, dancing the night away." Following his trusty cape's first venture at the Home Depot Center, it made several more cameo appearances. Pete says, "After that, I wore the cape for many shows and kind of got known a little for it—and, yes, ridiculed for it." For Pete, though, contending with the cape's few critics was worth it. To him, it signified what DMB shows are all about, which is "a huge celebration. Putting on that cape and not caring about anything else but having the best time in the world and listening to the best music in the world is the most important thing. I think part of me even wanted to inspire the people behind me. I mean, if you see a six-foot-two guy with superspiked hair, a headband, and a red cape dancing all night, how can you not have a good laugh?"

Fellow fans aren't the only ones who have had a good chuckle at the cape's expense. At the 2006 Hollywood Bowl show, even Dave himself got in on the joke. Pete laughs, remembering, "In between songs Dave came up to the mic, put on a really high-pitched voice and said, 'It's Superman! It's Superman!'" Though the cape has now been put into reserve for "special occasions," it has been captured for posterity on the *Live at Radio City* DVD, where Pete appears in the So Damn Lucky bonus section. It made its most recent cameo appearance at the superfan's hundredth show. When Dave saw Pete's "100th show! Thank you" sign, as Pete explains it, "he looked down and noticed my red cape, and his facial expression changed when he recognized who I was. He got this big smile on his face and gave me a nice head nod." Pete plans to bring the cape back out of semiretirement for his hundred and fiftieth show.

LEROI HOLLOWAY MOORE

IF I DIE BEFORE MY TIME

In the absence of a Charlottesville booking on the 2008 tour, the June 28, 2008, show in Bristow, Virginia, marked the closest DMB would come to a hometown show. Though it was still early in the tour, 2008 was already shaping up to be a good one, with Tim Reynolds adding an invigorating new energy and the band playing tight shows with mixed set lists and quite clearly having a lot of fun onstage. Just a few weeks in, they had already hit some major venues, including Susquehanna Bank Center in Camden, New Jersey; the New England Dodge Music Center in Hartford, Connecticut; and SPAC. Though the June 28 set list wasn't particularly out of the ordinary, it did feature the band debut of the cover of Peter Gabriel's "Sledgehammer" and the encore ended with another cover, Sly & the Family Stone's "Thank You." One fan, Jeff Roberts, in Bristow that night, remembers, "Little did we know the kind of show that would be. The set list was amazing, and the energy was high. It was as if they all knew. I remember Roi taking off his sunglasses and showing his face to the DMB world one last time. I get chills thinking about it."

Though the mainstream media often tended to focus primarily on Dave, from day one, those who saw DMB play live were acutely aware of the fact that Dave Matthews Band was just as much about the band as it was about Dave Matthews. While the members of DMB have always maintained low-key public profiles, over the years fans had become intimately familiar with the distinct presence and personality each one of the members brought to the stage. In many ways, onstage LeRoi Moore stood apart from his more boisterous bandmates. Whereas Carter was always grinning and highly interactive and Boyd would pounce to center stage in a cascade of flying braids, slicing into his violin, LeRoi spent much of his time standing still and quiet on stage left, most often wearing dark sunglasses that made it impossible to discern much of an expression. He often seemed to be waiting out the music, and then, at just the right moment, he would raise a horn to his lips and slide effortlessly into the music, reminding everyone that he was there. Sometimes he would do so with bellowing notes, but he also had a knack for "whispering"; at just the right moment, he would lay back into his horn, releasing quiet, captivating sounds.

And so it was in Bristow that night, just as it had been on pretty much every other night for the past seventeen years. Kim Zaepfel, in attendance that evening, remembers, "It was a show like any other at Nissan—sticky, hot, and the traffic was backed up everywhere. There were no expectations for the show other than we knew the band was playing and it was going to be great. We had amazing seats, and I remember looking at my husband, Bobby, as the band took the stage and saying, 'Holy crap! Roi looks great! Look how much weight he's lost!' Bobby agreed that Roi had never looked better. For probably the first time, we really heard Roi and Rashawn gel and sound like a complete section." (The concert recording was released as *Live Trax, Vol. 14*; all proceeds from the sale of the album were donated to charities including the Charlottesville Music Resource Center and Boys & Girls Club of Charlottesville/Albemarle.)

Due to the proximity of the Bristow show to DMB's hometown and a couple days off between Bristow and the next show at Verizon Wireless Amphitheatre in Charlotte, North Carolina, band members were able to retire to their own homes for a couple days' rest. On the morning of June 30, LeRoi Moore took his ATV for a spin around his property. While riding, he hit a ditch that was covered by grass and the ATV flipped over. Later that day, the following announcement, titled "An Important Announcement from DMB," appeared on the home page of the band's website: "LeRoi Moore was injured today in an ATV accident on his farm outside Charlottesville, Virginia. LeRoi was immediately transported to the University of Virginia Health System for treatment where he remains in serious condition. Please join us all in wishing LeRoi a speedy and complete recovery. Beginning tomorrow in Charlotte, NC, Béla Fleck and the Flecktones saxophonist, Jeff Coffin, will be sitting in with Dave Matthews Band while LeRoi recovers."

Though no one knew exactly what kind of injuries LeRoi had sustained, rumors began hitting fan message boards that it was serious—that the sax man had punctured a lung. But the band continued on without skipping a single beat, playing its next show as scheduled in Charlotte on July 1. As DMB had announced the previous day, Flecktones saxophonist Jeff Coffin stood in for Moore and the show went on. Even in his absence, though, LeRoi still had a presence at the show. That night, the Charlotte crowd delivered the first of the summer's many "We want Roi!" chants. Despite the band's website notice, not everyone was aware of what had happened to LeRoi when they walked into the Charlotte show that evening. Matt McKibben remembers, "I didn't know about the accident because we were traveling. I happened to sit next to a guy who told me about Roi and said, 'Don't worry about it, it's going to be okay. Jeff Coffin is filling in.' And it was this moment of joy because rarity is everything in the DMB world, and it seemed like it would be such a rare thing. Jeff had sheet music on-stage, and there was a lot of back-and-forth between him and Rashawn. It was crazy because Coffin's a professional through and through, but he looked a bit frantic up there. So Rashawn would nod to Jeff, and he would just go. It was crazy to watch because the songs Jeff didn't know, the parts where Roi would usually just be filler, Jeff, not knowing everything, would just tear into it."

Following the show, Stefan posted a message entitled "Stage Left Solidarity Coalition" on his MySpace page, which read, "Getting on stage without Leroi [sic] tonight was one of the hardest things for me to do in my history with this band. It felt I was missing my left arm. I kept thinking that he was there, but then he wasn't. I know that the love being sent his way will speed up his recovery and bring him back to the stage." That same night, the road crew posted a note on the Road page: "It's a day of swirling emotions out here on the road. We're immensely saddened by LeRoi's absence after his accident yesterday. After his first full day of recovery, we're learning that his condition is improving. Dave and Carter spent a few hours at his side this morning, laughing together and talking. He's alert and cracking jokes already. They commented on how much they were heartened and excited after leaving the hospital, knowing that he's going to be alright. Dave announced to the audience tonight 'He was beat up real good, but he's going to be fine.' Jeff Coffin has really stepped up to the plate. We are honored that he chose to drop everything at the last minute to fly out and sit in during Roi's time away. Jeff sat in a room with Rashawn all afternoon, learning parts. We were all amazed at how well he did tonight. A true professional. We're keepin' on with the keepin' on. See y'all in Raleigh tomorrow. Get well LeRoi . . . We love ya!"

And so it continued in much the same vein for several weeks. Crowds would chant for LeRoi; Dave would sometimes share a bit about Moore's progress with audiences; the official DMB website would offer up news about his condition as it alternately improved or worsened throughout July; the road crew would reference LeRoi at the end of each night's set list; and fans were invited to extend get-well wishes through e-mail and snail mail. There was an understanding among the fan base that LeRoi would not return for the remainder of the 2008 tour, though that had never been explicitly stated. In the meantime, Moore's decision to bring trumpeter Rashawn Ross on board two years earlier paid off in spades, and Jeff Coffin continued to fill in for LeRoi (with the exception of the August 5 Riverbend Music Center show in Cincinnati, for which Coffin had a conflicting engagement and DMB played sans saxophonist). For the most part, things sounded promising, with the exception of a July 18 announcement on the DMB website that Moore had been readmitted to the hospital.

But in the moments before the house lights went down at the Staples Center in Los Angeles on August 19, 2008, a strange vibe permeated the air. Although some of those in attendance were oblivious, others already knew that just a few hours before, the face of DMB had unexpectedly and irrevocably changed forever.

Earlier that afternoon, rumors had popped up on online message boards that LeRoi Moore had passed away. Though LeRoi's injury was clearly public knowledge by this point, it was commonly believed that he was healing while off the road for the remainder of the summer tour. So it was shocking when foreboding messages started to appear on DMB fan message boards. At first, many of the posts were met with disbelief—particularly because DMB was slated to play Staples that night and there was no word that the show had been canceled. But as the hours went by, the online messages gained more and more speed, until finally Moore's death was officially announced on CNN and then on the official DMB website. By that evening, DMB's website directed to a black page with an image of LeRoi that read simply, "In Memory of LeRoi Moore

(1961–2008)." Pete Paszkowski remembers the evening well. "There was a barrage of phone calls and texts. I think it was the shock of the fact that he passed away—I knew it was true, but I couldn't believe it. I didn't want to." An official statement from DMB confirmed the tragic news: "We are deeply saddened that LeRoi Moore, saxophonist and founding member of Dave Matthews Band, died unexpectedly Tuesday afternoon, August 19, 2008, at Hollywood Presbyterian Medical Center in Los Angeles from sudden complications stemming from his June ATV accident on his farm near Charlottesville, Virginia. LeRoi had recently returned to his Los Angeles home to begin an intensive physical rehabilitation program."

Brenda Gonzalez remembers, "I was at Staples, and I kept saying, 'If he had died, wouldn't they have canceled the show?' There weren't any signs, nothing. No one seemed to know anything about it." She continues, "We sat down, and I'm trying to wrap my head around how they're going to play. I'm wondering why they don't just cancel the show. We're talking to our neighbors—some of them knew, some of them didn't. Then DMB came out and they looked like hell, which, of course, you would expect."

For anyone in attendance who didn't know that tragedy had befallen DMB earlier that afternoon, it soon became abundantly clear. The band opened with a heartwrenching version of "Bartender" that included a sorrowful interpolation of "If I Only Had a Brain," one of their single most powerful song performances of all time. After the song came to an end, Dave stepped up to the microphone and announced, "We all had some bad news today. Due to some complications since some injuries he received earlier this summer, our good friend LeRoi Moore passed on and gave his ghost up today. And we will miss him forever." Though it was in some ways incomprehensible that DMB's remaining members had found the strength to go onstage just a few hours after learning of LeRoi's death, Mike Rofe remembers that there was a very special energy in Staples that night. "It felt like the whole crowd was together as one tight community."

Eric Wilder, also at Staples that night, remembers, "As the show progressed the band was really feeding off of the crowd. It started off really sad and slow with 'Bartender,' then 'Proudest Monkey' and 'So Damn Lucky,' and then progressed to 'The Maker' and 'Loving Wings.' There was an evolution to the point where they ended with 'Ants' and 'Two Step.' It was amazing to be a part of because you could see the band picking up."

Dan Williams remembers the evening vividly: "I was lucky enough to see LeRoi play at one of his last shows on June 6 in Chicago. That night opened with an amazing 'Dreaming Tree' that he and Rashawn truly tore up. But, for me, the highlight of the night was the return of 'Long Black Veil,' in which Roi took one of the most beautiful solos I can remember ever hearing him play. It was truly breathtaking. Three months later, I vividly remember signing in to WeeklyDavespeak.com and seeing the thread that Roi had passed. My heart sank. I didn't know what to think. But then, as a testament to his character, people who had never posted anything on the forums in that site posted here and there about their own memories of Roi. They began sharing their thoughts on his life and love of music. People who hadn't been on the site in years came back. All because of this man that they loved. We all, not just as a Weekly Davespeak community but a DMB community, came together that day and looked toward the future of DMB. What must have been the hardest day of the band members' lives was nothing short of devastating for the thousands and thousands of DMB faithful."

In addition to an immediate and profound outpouring of emotion from DMB's fan base, many fellow musicians expressed their sorrow about the loss of LeRoi as well. Kenny Chesney sang a rendition of "Where Are You Going" in honor of Moore; John Mayer dedicated his August 20 show to the sax player; the Allman Brothers dedicated "No One to Run with Anymore" to LeRoi at their SPAC show; Béla Fleck and the Flecktones, O.A.R., and Blues Traveler's John Popper all publicly expressed their sadness over the loss of Moore.

On Phish's website, Trey Anastasio remembered an onstage moment with Moore: "When Phish played Virginia Beach in 1997, LeRoi came on stage and started playing three saxophones at once and set off the most hilarious chain of events. Within minutes Page was playing four of his keyboards with his hands and feet and I had three guitars on and drumsticks in my hand banging on Fish's drums. And Mike was playing two basses. It was just a phenomenal moment! And I remember LeRoi laughing with his mouth full of saxophones." On August 21, RollingStone.com quoted Steve Lillywhite as saying "[LeRoi] was very much the king of a lot of things he did. I have great memories of staying up late in the studio working on music collages with him. He was a beautiful person. He had music—music was the number one thing for him."

Lillywhite's sentiment is one that Roi's remaining bandmates have echoed time and time again. LeRoi Moore *was* music. For as unassuming as he may have sometimes appeared onstage, he was anything but in the studio. Just as much as anyone else, LeRoi *was* DMB; aside from his own contributions on the horn, he also cowrote and arranged many of the songs in DMB's library. Of Moore, Matthews told *Relix* magazine in May 2009, "His musical instincts were really like no one else I'd ever met in my life." In the same interview, Carter Beauford said of his bandmate and lifelong friend LeRoi, "He was a horn player, but he had a rhythmical thing going on as well. Sometimes he would blow a solo that would be so percussive that, to me, it was almost like another drummer over there."

Aside from the loss of a staggeringly talented musician, for those who had built such a big part of their lives around DMB—who had found solace in the band's music and spent summer after summer traveling to shows—there were suddenly big question marks. Despite guest musicians such as Butch Taylor and Rashawn Ross, DMB was and had always been Dave, LeRoi, Carter, Stefan, and Boyd. What would happen now without Moore's saxophone, which was such a signature part of the quintessential

DMB sound? For perhaps the first time ever, everything seemed rather uncertain. Steven Boyette says, "After LeRoi died, there was a part of me that flashed to: What if this is the end? And if it is, what is my life going to look like moving forward? It's been caught up for so long in this thing. How would I adjust? What would I do with all this time?"

Unbelievable as it seemed at the time, not only did DMB manage to go onstage the evening of LeRoi's death, it also finished out the remainder of the summer 2008 tour (including four of shows in South America following the U.S. tour), with the exception of two canceled shows in Sacramento, California, and Salt Lake City, Utah, to accommodate Moore's funeral. (In compensation for two consecutively canceled Salt Lake City gigs—the first due to Moore's death in 2008 and the second in 2009 because of Matthews's strained vocal chords—DMB hosted a free show at USANA Amphitheatre on August 17, 2010.) In retrospect, however, the band's decision to play on makes perfect sense. In July 2009, Matthews told *Relix* magazine, "At least we knew we had one thing we had to do: we had to finish the tour because he would have. Not to say I know his thoughts, but what else are we gonna do? We're musicians." Though the band was noticeably shaken for the remainder of the tour, the shows that immediately followed LeRoi's death were some of the most moving and memorable in DMB history. Songs such as "Bartender," "So Damn Lucky," "Gravedigger," "Proudest Monkey," "The Maker," and "#41" were fitting tributes to LeRoi and frequently in rotation during those final 2008 shows. Every show at the Gorge Amphitheatre in George, Washington (and again at the final show of the U.S. tour at the Greek Theatre in Berkeley, California, which fell on what would have been Moore's forty-seventh birthday), included a montage tribute for LeRoi set to the music of "#34" between the main set and the encore. Difficult as it must have been for the band to get up and play, audiences at the Gorge and the Greek were given the opportunity to mourn what they also felt to be their loss and to express their support of the band.

Throughout those final shows of 2008, fans came together to express their sorrow over LeRoi's passing and sympathy for the band. Chants for "Roi" were heard frequently, and signs commemorating him could be seen throughout parking lots and venues. On the first night of the three-night Gorge stand, many members of DMB looked visibly shaken by the loss of their fallen brother. The three-night Gorge run, always a peak event in the band's annual touring schedule, was especially meaningful that year as it marked DMB's first show following Moore's funeral. Midset that night, per a request by a small group of fans, the DMB crew projected a trifold picture of LeRoi onto the screens at the back of the stage following "Help Myself." Once the picture flashed on the screen, the audience on the lawn of the Gorge collectively sent thousands of glow sticks flying out into the dark night sky, creating an effect of myriad multicolored dragonflies. For about five minutes, the entire show stopped and the band watched as the audience chanted for LeRoi and kept the glowsticks flying high in the air, whizzing from one end of the amphitheater to the other. Thousands came together that night in an effort to support the band and express their sorrow over LeRoi's death.

A witness to the glowstick tribute that evening, Brad Adams, remembers it as an extremely powerful moment, "We were in seats on stage right. A lot of people were throwing little glowsticks around throughout the night. There was talk of singing 'Somewhere over the Rainbow' as a tribute, and nothing really materialized until all of a sudden we looked up on the hill. We heard a bit of a ruckus and saw the band looking up too. There was this one section up on the middle of the lawn that was just waving glowsticks and throwing them around. Then, probably within five seconds or so, they started to throw them to one another. Then literally probably another five seconds, and the entire venue was throwing them *everywhere*. It was one of those moments where it was, like, how did this even start? Everybody just kind of ran with it. And I think everybody was just kind of helpless. We wanted to show the band, we wanted to give a tribute to Roi, but nobody knew how. And once this started it was like, 'Holy crap. I can't believe I'm watching this.' We looked at the band members, and they just kind of paused and folded their arms and let it all unfold. And when they put the picture of Roi up, it intensified tenfold. When you looked around, there really wasn't a dry eye in the house. It was one of those sad/happy moments. We started picking up glowsticks and throwing them every which way and trying to take pictures. After a couple seconds of that, you just sort of realized, To hell with it. A picture or video isn't ever going to convey what's going on here right now. So we just stood there and enjoyed it. Then I looked up on the stage, and I saw Boyd. He had turned away from the crowd; you could tell he was crying pretty hard. That just killed us. Just to be there that night as it unfolded—Dave paused the show and let the glow-sticks fly for probably four or five minutes, but it seemed like an eternity. It was so cool. And then, once he kind of put a stop to it, everything settled down and the band busted into '#41.'"

Adams continues, "I just remember thinking, Holy shit! Did we just see that? The next two nights people tried to do it again and they couldn't. Everyone who was there on night one was like, 'No, we did it Friday. Just leave it alone. You're never gonna have that moment again.' Looking back, it was just *so* cool to be there. It was such a crappy time. Everyone was like, 'What's going to happen to Gorge? Are they even going to do Gorge?' After thinking about it awhile, I realized they had to do Gorge. They probably *needed* to do Gorge. That's one of those memories I will absolutely take to the grave with me."

Another fan, Kaila Doherty, also remembers the intensity of the Gorge opening night. "I remember Dave staring out into the crowd, completely speechless for what seemed like an eternity. You could just feel the pain in his eyes and the appreciation he had for all of his fans to go along with it. After going to dozens of shows, I've never experienced that much of an emotional connection as the band made with the audience that night. After the long pause, the band started up into what was the most emotional '#41' I have ever heard." Monika Sovine adds, "I remember seeing a sign someone had made: ROI IS HERE. GORGE = HEAVEN. That summed up the experience perfectly. Though the sun had set already, there was a faint glow in the western sky that barely illuminated the Gorge canyon below us. With the stars, the slight breeze of late summer bearing the crisp hints of approaching autumn, and the best band in the world, we stood there together reveling in our love for one of the finest musicians to have graced the stage."

Following the third night at the Gorge, the DMB crew wrote on the band's website, "We're missing our friend. To paraphrase Dave, it's been a strange and difficult week. It is evident that this profound sorrow is common between band, crew, and fans. The audiences here at the Gorge are making their feelings known. Their gestures of remembrance are felt on stage. These are shows of healing, companionship, and emotion."

But the sorrow was intermingled with moments of joy and release, particularly at the subsequent three-night Berkeley stand that closed out the tour. A few nights after the Gorge glowstick extravaganza, the crowd at Berkeley's Greek Theatre staged their own tribute to Moore. Prior to the night-three show, on what would have been LeRoi's forty-seventh birthday, a group of fans distributed liquid bubbles and wands to the audience. DMB opened with "Bartender," only to be greeted by a sea of bubbles floating out from the crowd, up to the stage, and out into the dusk. These fan-headed tributes were not limited to the United States. At the Rio de Janeiro concert on September 30, South American fans came together to formulate a tribute of their own. In the midst of an energetic performance of "#41," the crowd released a sea of white balloons into the air as a tribute to Roi. Rodrigo Simas remembers simply, "It was a beautiful moment."

What was it about this man who stood so quietly on stage left with his sunglasses often shielding him from the crowd that stirred the emotions of so many people who had never shared a single word with him? Fans describe LeRoi's reticence to step up to the front of the stage as a big part of his charm. It often seemed as though he spoke only through his horn, in subtle, beautiful melodies that were a big part of what drew many to DMB in the first place. Jeff Cunningham says, "Diving into some of the older studio stuff and listening to Roi melt away a sax solo, that's when I start to get really sad. This is an original member of the band and, as great as Jeff Coffin is, it's never gonna be the same sound. Roi is kinda lackadaisical—just the way he incorporates himself into the band is different. I'll miss that. I'll miss his shades and how he stepped out of the spotlight."

Bryan Narciso says that, for him, Moore was a big part of the DMB allure. "When I first got into the band, everybody loved Dave, everybody loved Carter, both for obvious reasons. But I always liked LeRoi. He was quiet, cool. The way he could fit into the music was perfect. He never overpowered, he just snuck in there with these beautiful, beautiful pieces of music. Coffin is one of the best saxophonists in the world, but he brings more thunder and loudness to the stage, as opposed to what Roi did. When Roi passed, I was pretty broken up. I'm thankful DMB carried on, and I think Roi would be proud."

In many ways, the tragedy and suddenness of Moore's death have brought with them a new appreciation for DMB. Alan Gonzalez says, "There's so much joy every single show now. I used to complain when they'd play songs I was sick and tired of. I just realized I shouldn't complain. You gotta enjoy every show, you never know what's going to happen next. After LeRoi passed I realized I shouldn't have complained—I should have enjoyed those moments. I took them for granted." "I think that's what Roi taught us," muses Kim Zaepfel. "Dance while you can."

Through the music and the continuation of DMB, Moore will always live on. Dan Williams explains, "So it is with the memories of Roi in summers past that I go to DMB shows now. Walking in the gates, going to find my seat, I know that I am about to see something that will keep me on a 'DMB high' for weeks to come. It is partly due to the man LeRoi Moore that this experience exists, and for this I will never forget him."

Of course, in addition to keeping Moore close by through the music, the experience has also given fans a newfound appreciation for the remaining band members who soldiered on and kept the music alive, even in their darkest hours. One fan, Kaysie Bowman, says that, for her, watching DMB work their way through this has been inspiring. "I admire the way DMB has grown over the past couple years during the great tragedy of losing LeRoi. A lot of bands would have packed it up and become just a memory—but not DMB. They were able to come together and build up from a dark place. I think that LeRoi would be very proud of his bandmates and brothers. I know I am very proud of them and thankful for the music they continue to make."

CHAPTER 8

LEROI'S LEGACY

DRINKING BIG WHISKEY WHILE WE DANCE AND SING

I t seemed as though LeRoi Moore's passing ignited a creative fire under the remaining band members. Almost immediately after soldiering through the end of the 2008 tour, which culminated with the four shows in South America, DMB returned to the studio with Rob Cavallo to fully realize some of the many jams and snippets they had created with Moore present in both Haunted Hollow and Seattle over the course of the past few years. This time, though, DMB went to an entirely new setting, holing up in Piety Street Recording in New Orleans. It was there, as Dave told *Relix* magazine in July 2009, that the band knew it had to "go and finish this recording that [LeRoi] knew was great. So we all went back into the studio thinking: *We can't fuck around.* Because this one is an ode."

Throughout the press for the album that ultimately came of those sessions, *Big Whiskey and the GrooGrux King,* Matthews has said that the decision to finish recording in New Orleans was based in part on LeRoi's love of the city. The band thrived in the sometimes gritty, sometimes festive, but always musical culture of the Big Easy. The location clearly colored the recording to some degree and is particularly evident on the song "Alligator Pie," a driving hoedown that references Hurricane Katrina, and also the tune "Squirm," which includes the voice of Mr. Okra, a somewhat legendary produce truck vendor and colorful New Orleans character.

Though LeRoi did not live to see the final sessions for *Big Whiskey*, by all accounts he played an integral role in constructing the initial jams that ultimately blossomed into a full album's worth of material. Moreover, because recording sessions had already occurred prior to his death, DMB was able to pick up several of Moore's horn licks and snippets and include them on the album—in fact, *Big Whiskey* both opens and closes with LeRoi's horns. In July 2009 Boyd Tinsley told *Relix*, "There was this big effort to find these parts and passages that Roi recorded and incorporate them." Additional horn fills were provided by Rashawn Ross and Jeff Coffin. Guitarist Tim Reynolds also joined DMB in the studio once again, returning for the first time since *Before These Crowded Streets*. Also included on *Big Whiskey* are guest spots by the Charlottesville banjo player Danny Barnes.

Though perhaps not explicitly addressed, Moore's death colors *Big Whiskey*'s lyrics. Following the whimsical opener, "Shake Me like a Monkey," the remainder of the album takes a darker turn, with weighty lyrics that address loss, death, and the state of mankind and the environment. As David Fricke wrote on RollingStone.com on June 2, 2009, "The sudden loss hangs over this record's startling punch like one of [New Orleans'] humid summer rains." There also appear to be several implicit dedications to Moore, such as "Lying in the Hands of God," a beautiful song that features a morose Matthews singing a duet in tandem with a lilting horn. The acoustic "Baby Blue" appears to serve as a serenade from Dave to LeRoi under the guise of a traditional love song.

More explicit is "Why I Am," which has gone on to serve as a rollicking tribute to LeRoi in live settings. The song evolved from a lick jammed out during earlier recording sessions that Moore was particularly fond of. The lyrics explicitly cite LeRoi in the chorus, referring to the saxophonist by his nickname, "Grux." Frequently introduced by Dave onstage as a tribute to LeRoi, audiences almost immediately took "Why I Am" into their own hands, and in concert the song generally features a crowd of thousands singing along in homage to LeRoi at the top of their lungs.

Clearly, the album's title also utilizes this GrooGrux reference. DMB actually stumbled upon the full album title during a promotional photo shoot in New Orleans, when a drunk vagrant asked the band for money for "big whiskey." Rashawn commented that "big whiskey" would be a good name for an album, and thus the complete title *Big Whiskey and the GrooGrux King* was born. In the documentary *The Road to Big Whiskey,* Dave explains, "I like as a full name *Big Whiskey and the GrooGrux King* because it sounds like a fairytale. Like a fairytale from New Orleans."

Finally, LeRoi is apparent even in the album's artwork. Dave, long known in fan circles for creating unique caricatures, began scribbling away and ultimately produced an intricate hand-drawn image that incorporated scenes inspired from various lyrics throughout the album, all occurring in the midst of a parade down what appears to be a French Quarter street. At the center of the parade is a giant face, which resembles Moore, atop a float. Many have speculated that this is a reference to traditional New Orleans jazz funerals, which are somewhat celebratory affairs, awash with music.

As opposed to the more elusive earlier days of *Big Whiskey*'s pre-production, fans were privy to a lot of information once the New Orleans sessions commenced. During the South American tour, Matthews started a Twitter account, which he continued to utilize regularly throughout the *Big Whiskey* sessions. Though fans were unaware of it at the time, he frequently sent out tweets that referenced lyrics and song names. Less vague tweets also let fans know that the band was in New Orleans, hard at work on the long-anticipated album.

In conjunction with what was originally expected to be an April 14, 2009, album release, DMB announced one of its longest tours to date. Beginning with a spring tour of the United States, which was to be quickly followed by a lengthy summer tour, breaking in the middle for a few weeks in Europe, then back across the pond to finish out the United States, DMB had a busy year ahead of it. In addition to touring members Tim Reynolds and Rashawn Ross, Jeff Coffin stepped in to fill in the gap left by LeRoi's death. The original intent was for the spring-tour Madison Square Garden opener in New York City to coincide with the release of *Big Whiskey*, but a couple months in advance it was announced that the album would be pushed back to June 2, with the first single, "Funny the Way It Is," releasing on April 14 via the band's official website and Pandora. Nonetheless, fans who attended the spring tour were provided with a preview of the album, through songs such as "Funny the Way It Is," "Seven," "Spaceman," "Why I Am," and "Beach Ball" (which appeared on a bonus CD in the *Big Whiskey* box set). During promotion, Dave frequently stated that the band had made a concerted effort not to take deadlines into account when it came to this album—it wanted to release the album *it* envisioned, when the music was ready.

The founder of dontburnthepig.org, Chris Urzi, remembers hearing three of these *Big Whiskey* songs played live for the first time at the Madison Square Garden spring-tour opener. "I was fortunate to have heard three of the thirteen *Big Whiskey* songs live for the very first time at Madison Square Garden. These songs were as good as hearing a new song being road tested because, aside from the 'Funny the Way It Is' single being released the same day as the show, none of these songs had been heard live or otherwise before that point. Earlier in the day, Dave posted a tweet offering a free download of the new single, and I listened to it a thousand times before the show. When I heard 'Funny the Way It Is' for the first time live, all I could think is, Well, it's got a catchy hook and what's not to love about Boyd's solo? 'Spaceman' was a cool, chill, mellow tune. Though I couldn't understand much of the lyrics at first aside from 'all the freaks are on parade' (which I love), Carter's riff was subtle but strong and it was very good to hear Rashawn standing out more prominently on these new songs. As for 'Why I Am,' it was an instant crowd-pleaser. How can you not start grooving to the guitar riff and lyrics to LeRoi? After DMB played the song for that first time, hearing the crowd chanting 'LeRoi, LeRoi' was absolutely bone-chilling."

Yet again, DMB utilized the latest music technology by launching its album promotion through Pandora, an Internet-based personalized radio program. In an April 16, 2009, press release, Pandora announced, "For the first time ever, an artist will be using Pandora and the Music Genome Project to introduce a new single and the new album, *Big Whiskey and the GrooGrux King*, directly to their fans." On a special Pandora site, fans could see special making-of videos and begin listening to a streaming version of the album a week prior to its official release.

Though fans had certainly waited a long time for this album—much longer than any other album to date, with a four-year gap between *Stand Up* and *Big Whiskey*—it appeared that the wait was worth it. Although *Big Whiskey* once again did not include any of the songs fans had grown accustomed to hearing over the previous summer tours (with the exception of "#27," which also appeared on the four-disc bonus CD), feedback on the new songs was generally positive following the spring tour. Matt McKibben says, "*Big Whiskey* is a monster. It's everything I've been waiting for. In my opinion, they made no sacrifices, they made no compromises. And considering they did it with bits and pieces of LeRoi . . . the story behind the album couldn't get any better. In my opinion, songs like 'Sugar Will' just don't belong on here. There's not a weak moment. Everything they should've done with that album, they did."

When the album finally did release on June 2, 2009, like McKibben, the vast majority of the DMB fan base was extremely pleased for the first time in several years. Although it certainly featured a more aggressive rock sound than the Big Three albums had, *Big Whiskey* was a definitive return to many of the elements that had made DMB's earlier albums so beloved: a prominent full-band sound, meaningful lyrics, and complex, intricate musicianship. Eric Wilder remembers his response to the release: "When I first listened to *Big Whiskey*, I realized the guys really delivered their best efforts on the album. Personally, I always find myself listening to DMB's live material much more often than studio albums, even in the case of the Big Three. While I value all that this band puts out, I think that most of their studio work cannot capture their true talent and uniqueness. When I first heard *Big Whiskey*, I immediately knew that this was a rare exception where I would prefer the album's studio cuts over live versions. Cavallo and the guys did an exceptional job of capturing the energy and emotion of the band, and the message is clear from the get-go with the 'Grux' segue into 'Shake Me Like A Monkey.' For me, that opening run through 'Why I Am' made me love this album upon first listen. In terms of production, *Big Whiskey* is my favorite DMB album because of the quality of work put into each song." Ultimately, Chris Urzi says, "Whatever your impressions of *Big Whiskey* are, one thing is clear: DMB was not going to stick to a script, and that is what makes this album and these songs so fun."

The band too was clearly very pleased with *Big Whiskey* and viewed the final product as one that LeRoi would be proud of. In July 2009 Dave told *Relix*, "[LeRoi's] musical instincts were really like no one else I'd ever met in my life. And [this] was already his favorite album, even though we hadn't finished. So that's the one great sorrow about this album—that he's not here for it. The whole process was incredibly genuine, which was something that Roi always talked about: 'All we need to be is honest.'"

Fans also appreciated *Big Whiskey* as a fitting farewell to LeRoi. One fan, Jared Smith, remembers, "The release of *Big Whiskey* brought a new wave of emotions. From the title to the album art, the songs he was featured on and the studio videos, everything was bittersweet. My first show that year in Alpharetta was my first since his passing—even though we saw the band the year before without Roi, it was different knowing he wouldn't be coming back, and it was very, very sad. But I could feel DMB celebrating his life in the *Big Whiskey* songs, and still every time the band plays 'Why I Am,' I tear up a little."

The *Big Whiskey* release was accompanied with much fanfare, including a four-part documentary on Fuse cable TV network and a Fuse/Hulu.com live broadcast of an album-debut show at New York City's Beacon Theatre. *Big Whiskey* opened at the top of the charts, providing DMB with its fifth consecutive number one debut, putting it into a small club with only four other artists to have ever achieved this feat. A little more than two months after its release, *Big Whiskey* was certified platinum.

Big Whiskey went on to be nominated for two Grammys: Album of the Year and Best Rock Album. (DMB did not win either category, with Album of the Year going to Taylor Swift's *Fearless* and Best Rock Album going to Green Day for *21st Century*.) Fittingly, the Grammy ceremony was held at Los Angeles' Staples Center, which marked the band's first return to the venue since the day of Moore's death in 2008. Many fans took issue with the Grammys, not because of DMB's loss in those two categories but because the previous year the awards broadcast had neglected to include LeRoi (a Grammy winner) in its in memoriam tribute. Fans made their disdain well known, both online and through direct calls and e-mails to the Recording Academy. In response, on February 10, 2009, the Recording Academy released a statement: "Nearly 250 members of our music community have passed in the last year, and all of them have been listed in the program book for the 51st Annual GRAMMY Awards, including LeRoi Moore. For the Encore segment of our annual GRAMMY Awards telecast, unfortunately we are unable to include all of the talented and wonderful people within the allotted timeframe." *Rolling Stone* got in on the Grammy oversight as well, writing on February 11, 2009, "Dave Matthews Band fans who tuned in for Sunday night's Grammy Awards were livid, and with good reason. . . . Despite the Grammy's excuse, the omission of Moore, who won a Grammy in 1997 with the rest of DMB for 'So Much To Say,' is a major oversight."

The year 2009 was a blur of promotional appearances and media hits. Throughout, DMB was particularly open about discussing the trials and tribulations that had plagued it in preceding years—to the extent that, unbeknown to fans at the time, the group had teetered on the verge of a breakup. The band itself has always been private about this difficult period.

In a 2009 interview with CBS *Sunday Morning*, Matthews remembers some of those dark times, when he was tired of fronting the band that bore his name. He says it was LeRoi who really pushed him to "be a leader" and live up to his role as the front man of the band—asking him to step up and heal the strife that was tearing the band apart. Dave says that, despite Moore's warnings, he had "sent everybody a letter, which was the opposite of being a leader, and said 'I can't handle it anymore.' It just wasn't fun. At that point we weren't communicating, and it was just sort of bitter. . . . If you're in a relationship with people, little things become big things; big things become little things." When questioned further about the letter, Matthews replied, "It was fairly final." All of a sudden, all the starts and stops over the past few years began to make a bit more sense. In the same CBS interview Carter Beauford further explained, "There were some turbulent times. For years, actually. But that's all part of it."

In the documentary *The Road to Big Whiskey*, Stefan Lessard described

Stand Up as "the change of what was happening musically with the guys in the band. We became a little bit more distant from each other, and the music that was once really easy to make with each other started to become difficult. . . . We didn't hit the bottom—but we saw the bottom. And the bottom meant no more band."

All of the band members were clear, however, that not only had all problems been resolved prior to Moore's death, but also that the sax player had played a crucial role in keeping the band together. Stefan explained in *The Road to Big Whiskey,* "We've had so many ups and downs in this band. But we were at an all-time high last year. Before the tour we were in the studio, and we were all together."

With the troubled times behind them, the band was ready to move on, taking its new music across even greater expanses than ever before. The years 2009 and 2010 were a particularly victorious period not only for DMB but also for European fans, who had always fallen somewhat by the wayside. In 2009 DMB played to varied audiences in Europe, including some extremely large crowds at music festivals and other much smaller ones at its own headlining shows. In addition to the tour, the official DMB website opened a European store (2010) and released both a *Europe 2009* box set and a *Live Trax* release of the Lucca, Italy, show.

DMB's last foray to Europe in 2007 had been limited, with a total of only five shows, none of them in Italy. So for Italian fans, the July 5, 2009, Lucca show was the first time DMB had played their country since 1998. An American fan, Mike Leone, made the trip across the pond to attend the show and remembers that, though he didn't know what to expect going in, he ended up witnessing a truly memorable spectacle.

"The piazza was small, surrounded by four buildings with a statue in the middle. The stage was massive—it looked like it could have gone into

Soldiers Field—but the piazza was tiny. Five thousand people tops were in this area." Because the show took place in a public area, Leone got to see DMB's crew setting up the band equipment, something that is always behind the scenes in the large amphitheaters and stadiums American audiences know. "I've never gotten to sit there and watch the crew set up. I've never gotten to see the two hours it takes to haul Carter's drum kit out of the crate and set it up from start to finish. To see it all was unbelievably cool. I have a lot of respect for the crew because they're not famous; they're just behind the scenes all the time and probably work harder on a day-to-day basis than the band. At one point, Stefan walked out on the stage with his camera to go wander around and check out the town. He could never just saunter out like that at Alpine. But there I think everyone just thought he was part of the crew."

Once the show started, Leone says, it was clear that the crowd was in for something special. The combination of the Italian audience's eleven-year wait for DMB, the band's energy, and the unique piazza setting created the perfect scenario. "When DMB walked onstage, I would compare the energy in that small Italian piazza to what it's like in Madison Square Garden. It was incredible. Every single band member seemed taken aback—as they looked out at the crowd, it was kind of like they were registering 'Holy shit!' They proceeded to put on one of the best performances I've ever seen in terms of music, passion, and energy—the band was just jumping up and down all over the place. It was truly remarkable. They went thirty minutes over curfew that night, doing a double encore. It was so clear the band was feeling it; it was for the fans that night. The entire piazza was just crazy from start to finish.

"After the show," Leone continues, "I just kind of sat down and was in awe. For someone like me who's seen DMB play some of the best shows of their career at MSG, Red Rocks, the Gorge, and Alpine to come away knowing I've witnessed a top-five show is kind of miraculous. It was truly one of these magical, onetime, special performances that can never be repeated. These people had longed for DMB to come back for so long, they had two-day celebrations in the countryside prior to the show. The stage was set, and it was set by a million different forces that will never be repeated."

Though the Lucca show was a rowdy one, generally speaking, European audiences tend to be quite different from their American counterparts. Corsina Andriano, a staff member of the Italian DMB fan organization Con-Fusion, says, "American and European shows are two completely different worlds. In my opinion, the real difference is the different approach to music. Italians are a demanding audience as far as the music is concerned, and they love to *listen* to good music in general. For us Italians, to attend a DMB concert is a precious rarity. So we love and respect what is happening musically, and we often listen in silence because we are enthralled by what happens onstage. At Italian shows, the music is at the core of the event; at U.S. shows, the atmosphere is festive, and for many the actual concert seems to be only one of the ingredients of the party." The cofounder of the website Dave Matthews Band UK, Kyri Karaiskakis, believes that, at least in the United Kingdom, because fans have fewer opportunities to see DMB play, they tend to be less opinionated than their American counterparts when it comes to set list choices. This is not to say, however, that watching DMB is a bystander sport across the pond. During the winter 2010 U.K. stops, Karaiskakis says, "DMB brought back 'Sugar Will' in London, which was amazing to see. 'Big Eyed Fish' was teased at the Birmingham show. Both these songs came back into circulation as a result of signs brought by fans."

Indeed, there are many differences between the American and international DMB experiences, primarily due to the band's historic concentration on domestic shows. Although DMB's first European tour occurred fairly early on in its career (March 1995), in the time since then its presence in Europe and other international stages has been sporadic at best, though certainly more frequent since 2007. Though some international fans caught on to DMB either through one of the band's intermittent ventures outside the United States, their own visits to the United States, or tapes or word of mouth from American friends, DMB has never enjoyed consistent high-profile airtime internationally. Nonetheless, a grassroots following has emerged in Europe and South America, much as it did in the early days in the United States.

In many ways, the international DMB community mirrors the American fan base of the early 1990s. With little to no airplay, depending upon the country, DMB is a group that most international fans stumble upon either by word of mouth or through some sort of fluke. Karaiskakis says, "I can only think of one DJ that plays DMB [in the United Kingdom]: Bob Harris on Radio 2. The band seems to be spreading a bit more with consecutive European tours, but people still mainly hear about them through word of mouth." International venues tend to be much smaller than their American counterparts, with seating capacities in the low thousands. In many ways, this affords Europeans a distinctive experience; over there it's still possible to see DMB play in settings far more intimate than the amphitheaters, stadiums, and ballparks America knows. It also gives the band a chance to do what it does best but rarely has the opportunity to do in the United States at this point: win over new audiences. This combination has lent itself to some unique and intimate experiences that most American fans will never get to enjoy.

International fan clubs have banded together to help one another build DMB communities with the goal of bringing DMB to international audiences on a more frequent basis. Rodrigo Simas of Brazil started one of the earliest organized international DMB communities with his website DMBrasil.net. Simas first caught on to DMB when it played with Ben Harper in Brazil in 1998. "I was already a Ben Harper fan but had never heard about DMB. Seeing them live with zero expectations transformed my life," he remembers. Inspired, he launched DMBrasil.com in November 2000. Based on his experience launching and growing DMBrasil.com, Simas always offers a helping hand when other sites such as Italy's Con-Fusion need assistance. As DMB has increased its visibility throughout Europe with back-to-back tours in summer 2009 and winter 2010, more and more organized fan clubs have started popping up in countries including the United Kingdom, Argentina, Portugal, and France. "It's just the right thing to do," says Simas about assisting in the development of websites for DMB fan clubs in other countries. "I helped start up Con-Fusion in Italy, and now it has the strongest community in Europe. I feel like I did my part in it, and that's nice. I am up for anything to help spread DMB music across the globe—I am more than happy to help everyone out."

Internationally, fans have interacted with the band in various ways. Simas, for example, experienced every fan's dream come true when he actually got to create the set list for DMB's Rio de Janeiro show on September 30, 2008 (released as *Live Trax, Vol. 19*). "I was having some caipirinhas [classic Brazilian alcohol drinks] with Dave and the guys after the São Paulo show, and Dave turned to me and said, 'Hey, write down some songs that you think the fans would like to hear in Rio and bring it to the show.' I thought he was just being nice to me. Anyway, I wrote two lists: 'My Set List' and 'Other Fan Favorites.' Two hours before the show, we were eating and Dave and Carter were next to me and I said, 'Hey, here are the songs you asked for.' Dave looked at it for a minute, talked to Carter about the song order, then turned to me again and asked if he could change a couple of songs. You should have seen my face. I was thinking, You can change anything you want, you crazy dude, still not believing that he was really thinking about using my set list. But that night the band really *did* play my set. I think it was one of the moments, as a fan, that I felt the most honored to do what I do with DMBrasil."

In part because of this greater accessibility and the chance to see

DMB play more intimate venues abroad, Kyri Karaiskakis says he doesn't necessarily want to see DMB reach the same heights of recognition it has achieved in America. "Many of us here would like to keep DMB as a well-kept secret as it offers us more opportunities to see the band in small, intimate venues and meet the band in very relaxed circumstances. DMB is not heard on the radio or found in record shops over here. To find DMB, you have to look for them." That may not be the case for long, though. According to a fellow U.K. fan, Evan Schiff, who has been following DMB since 1996, "When I first moved to the U.K. two years ago, I felt like a missionary trying to convert people over here. It was hard for people to get a true sense of DMB's worth without the band consistently touring Europe. Now it seems that's all changing."

After returning to Europe yet again in the winter of 2010, it was time for DMB to turn an eye toward the U.S. summer tour. Ironically, though, before the 2010 tour even began, everyone's attention turned toward 2011. On May 14, 2010, DMB released a statement on its website entitled "A Message to Our Fans": "As we feel the excitement building for this summer, we wanted to let everyone know that after twenty years of consecutive touring, Dave Matthews Band will be taking 2011 off. We feel lucky that our tours are a part of so many people's lives, and wanted to give everyone as much notice as possible. We're excited to make this summer one of our best tours yet, and look forward to returning to the road in 2012."

For the vast majority of major touring bands today, tour-related announcements pertain to shows that *will* be happening, as opposed to those that will not. But for DMB, which had not spent anything close to a full year off the road in the two decades since its inception in 1991, this was massive news. For so many fans who have an entrenched tradition of spending their summer months hitting shows across the nation, this break would be uncharted territory.

Brad Adams, who has been going to shows since 1996, remembers his friends' reaction to the announcement: "Everyone's like, 'Damn it! What are we gonna do?' That was the first question: Where should we go? What should we do? As far as 2011 goes for DMB, well deserved. I mean, how many bands have been out there for twenty years on the same scale as them? Nobody. For DMB to do what they did for so long and to tell us now, to acknowledge they're a big part of our lives . . . the fact they're at least warning us is cool. Instead of just pulling the plug at the last minute and saying 'Nah, we're not gonna do it this year.' I feel like that's respect to the fans."

And so the 2010 tour began with even more anticipation than usual; audiences were acutely aware they had to make the summer count more than ever before. Again with Tim Reynolds, Rashawn Ross, and Jeff Coffin in tow, DMB kicked the season off in Hartford, Connecticut, on May 28, by immediately breaking down walls and resurrecting tunes from deep in the band's catalog. One after another, five songs were "liberated" that evening, with rarities such as "Hello Again," "Kit Kat Jam," and "Busted Stuff" re-emerging, seemingly out of nowhere. (DMBAlmanac.com tracks the band's played songs. Any song that has not been played for 1,000 days or more is placed on the Liberation List until it reemerges.) As if that weren't enough, DMB ended the show with the debut of "Break for It" in the encore. Fans had previously been aware of this song's existence only because of sound-check recordings from 2006; in the years since then, the song had never been played publicly. Stefan cites that first night at Hartford as including one of his favorite moments in the band's history to date, when the audience spontaneously jumped in and took over the lead vocals on "Dancing Nancies."

Throughout the course of 2010, the band continued in that vein, frequently shocking audiences with the inclusion of songs that had been abandoned for years at a stretch like "The Last Stop" (which had been the subject of much chanting for years on end), "Good, Good Time," and "Minarets." All told, by the end of the summer tour, DMB had dug deep into their catalog, liberating a total of nineteen songs. This nearly doubled the amount of songs liberated in any prior touring year, with the second-highest number of liberations topping off at ten in 2006. In many ways it seemed as though the band had decided that if they were going to take a break in 2011, they were going to go out in style. Long after DMB's initial tour dates were announced, more stops kept being added to the schedule, including a two-night stand at Chicago's Wrigley Field, four stops in South America, and a nine-city fall tour. Nineteen years into DMB's career, not only did the band have the third-highest-grossing North American tour (with 1,270,477 tickets sold in North America—this does not account for European and South American ticket sales), but the 2010 run also marked the band's most diverse outing to date. In addition to all the liberated songs, upon the summer tour's conclusion the stat-tracking website DMBAlmanac.com wrote, "Returns and one-offs were the themes of the tour and why this tour will be remembered. In fact, the band played 94 different songs. . . . This destroyed the previous high of 75 in summer 2008 . . . they also performed over 1,000 different songs [in one touring year] for the first time."

Of this willingness to experiment within their catalog Stefan says, "At this point in our career we've been around for twenty years. We're not supporting a record at the moment, we already did *Big Whiskey* support last year and worked on getting those songs to a rocking, hitting place. You know, 'Time Bomb,' when we first started playing it, almost felt a little bit contrived to me, like we were trying to be Led Zeppelin or something. But now it's to a place where I feel like it's ours, we own it, and we can play it to full intensity. As for the older songs, we're at a point where we're not planning a new record at the moment. So there are all these open options."

Some of the band's increasingly pronounced willingness to experiment onstage may also be due to the traveling rehearsal room that was incorporated into the 2010 tour. For the first time, rather than doing sound checks in a relatively public setting, DMB created a portable space where the members could gather together in private to jam on a daily basis, garage-band style. According to Stefan, the potential for the rehearsal room to have an impact on experimentation is significant. "I've been trying to get Dave to bring back 'Crazy-Easy' now for three years. It's a hard one because it's one of the ones where I don't think he was feeling it even when we were writing it. So it's hard if a song just feels like it never should have been started, it's hard to want to bring it out. So I think that's the case with a lot of songs we have that you don't hear a lot of. 'Good, Good Time' is another one that I keep trying to throw out there. Dave always liked that song, but I believe there were some problems with the arrangements—it was so loose that certain other people in the band had a hard time putting their heads around it. If everyone's not behind it, you get a very wishy-washy thing. I think with this rehearsal room, things like this will change."

Lessard has gained a reputation in the DMB community as something of a man of the people through his years of online communication with fans and his understanding of the desire for the liberation of songs like "Good, Good Time" and "Crazy-Easy." He has developed a one-on-one conversation of sorts with fans—one that often gravitates toward fans relying on "Fonz" to be their advocate in getting the band to bring "missing" songs back into the set-list rotation. "There was something I was longing for in the music and the sets of the band, and I think it was the same things the fans were looking for," Stefan explains of the role he's grown into. "So I don't mind playing to that. I enjoy throwing things out there. I recently threw out the idea of doing a full-length album at a show. The amount of positive response to that was incredible. And I wasn't too sure what the response was going to be. I wasn't sure if people would think that was too cheesy or if we weren't the type of band they'd want to see do that."

The cyberaccess to the fan base Lessard has developed over the years has allowed him to act as a bridge of sorts between the band and the fan community—two circles that are inherently separate yet intricately connected. "Using the fans as a guide is like a library for me," Stefan explains. "For example, we played 'Cornbread' into 'Stand Up,' and people just didn't really dig it very much," he remembers of the May 29, 2010, Hartford show. "The next night we did 'Cornbread' into 'Recently.' That was an idea I had . . . so we threw out 'Recently' and everyone was psyched on that segue." The fans know the band is listening and seem to take extra pleasure in the shows when they know their feedback is being heard and responded to.

But of course, in this community, any number of versions of these old, neglected songs are just a few mouse clicks away. With twenty years' worth of live recordings easily accessible, there is always more to be discovered and discussed. Despite the trials and learning curves that have occurred throughout the past twenty years as DMB has rolled with the tide of changing music-sharing practices, one great benefit that cannot be disputed has emerged—namely, accessibility. The vast majority of DMB's lifetime of shows is now just a mouse click away. And although the community has lost part of its foundation with the death of the B&P process, in some ways the increased accessibility of the DMB archive has reinvigorated the fan base.

With so much music spanning such a great expanse of time, it's always possible to unearth a forgotten show or find a new version of a familiar song. And with a band like DMB, where even the most time-tested and staple songs are in a constant state of evolution, music sharing allows things to stay fresh. Jake Vigliotti muses, "Look at the song 'Two Step.' DMB has been playing that song for basically twenty years. You can go back to 1992 and listen to 'Two Step' and listen to a 'Two Step' from 2009, and they're totally different songs. Sure, it's the same song, but the lyrics and jams are completely different. That's one of the things that's totally unique about this band."

The ability of DMB to constantly change things up has played a large role in keeping tapers engaged as well, even today, despite the significant time and expense involved. John Kelly points out, "A lot of bands outside of DMB play the same set list every night. If tonight's show in Richmond is just like the show in Charlotte last night, I'm not sure I want to tape it. After all, I'm not going to get anything different." This is compounded by DMB's sense of spontaneity, which also contributes to the draw for tapers. Because it's always possible for a new jam to be played, a long-forgotten song to be pulled out of the archives, or a spur-of-the-moment burst of crowd-band interaction to spring up, tapers always run the very real chance of being there to capture and preserve a special and unique moment.

Better technology has also given new life to old shows that were either never released in the first place or were lost over time, as so many of the shows were in the early days of cassettes, and especially in the transition from cassette to CD format. So not only has online music sharing made shows more accessible, but, combined with digital audio technology, it has essentially expanded the fan-generated DMB archive.

Due largely to increased recording technology and accessibility, archiving began to emerge as a DMB trading niche as the 2000s progressed. With the dawn of sites such as DMBAlmanac.com, a portion of the fan base became more and more interested in tracing back to old shows—determining lost set lists and finding recorded versions of rare or now-obsolete shows. As a result, old cassette traders who held on to their collections became sources for missing or hard-to-find information.

One taper and self-proclaimed DMB archivist, Tom "Rockinman" Gambichler, has become somewhat of an expert on this topic. Over the past few years, Gambichler has spent countless hours converting old tapes that either never hit the trading circuit or were of extremely low quality into clean digital form and reconverting early CDs to lossless digital format. Because some of the shows are difficult to identify based on long-ago mislabeled tapes and a lack of clear set-list sources for DMB's earlier gigs, Gamblicher listens carefully to the recordings, then sweeps old mailing lists such as Minarets Digest in an attempt to identify prompts and clues that will definitively identify the shows in question. The shows are then verified on DMBAlmanac.com and etree.org before they are put up for mass consumption on Dreamingtree.org.

With the launch of the *DMB Live* series in 2008, the band too began contributing to the resurrection of older, more difficult to get shows. Although it is not specifically limited to DMB's earlier days, shows released in this series tend to concentrate on the early to mid-'90s, including rarities such as Dave and Tim's 1993 acoustic set at the Prism Coffeehouse in Charlottesville and the 1992 full-band show at Washington, D.C.'s Bayou. In a nod to the changing times, the releases in this series are available only in digital format, with no CD option.

With twenty years of evolving music to sample from and an ever-increasing sense of nostalgia for the early days, a certain sector of the DMB community has become historians of sorts. Older recordings that were previously difficult to come by or lost altogether serve a great sentimental purpose for longtime fans once they reemerge on the digital circuit. Andy Svenson says, "For a person who was actually at that show in 1995 or 1996, getting their hands on a recording of the show is invaluable."

Even today, when DMB has achieved mainstream and commercial success, taped live recordings play a large role in the band's continued upward trajectory and in uniting and promoting the ongoing engagement of the community. At this point, taping and trading (in whatever form they may take) are an integral part of the whole experience for DMB fans. Looking back, Svenson muses, "If the trading wasn't a part of it, I don't think I would have become as big of a fan or be following them as much as I do today. I followed a lot of other bands around the time I found DMB—but I can't say that I think about those other bands much anymore. It definitely gives you a greater appreciation for the band, being able to go back to the recordings from the 1990s, just to see where they've come from and how they're still evolving."

Though fans ended 2010 braced for DMB's 2011 break, on January 19, 2011 it was announced that, despite the band's earlier statement that they would be taking the year off, 2011 would not be completely barren as previously expected. In a statement simply titled "Summer 2011" the band wrote: "2011 is our 20th anniversary as a band and we want to celebrate by playing music together. While we are still taking the year off from touring, we have decided to plan four multi-day, multi-artist music events that will take place this summer."

Although the lack of a complete tour certainly represents a deviation from the normal summer-long tour fans have become so accustomed to over the years, these unexpected 2011 shows seem fitting. After two decades, DMB and its fans will celebrate this twenty-year milestone the way they've done everything else up to this point—together.

HITTING THE ROAD

WOULD YOU LIKE TO DANCE AROUND THE WORLD WITH ME?

Though online activity has certainly been a driving force behind DMB, ultimately everything begins and ends with the shows. For the vast majority of DMB fans, it's the concerts that got them hooked on the band in the first place and the shows that keep them coming back year after year. And it's not only the shows themselves but the anticipation and dissection of them that keep the community churning all year long. DMB set the tone for the culture of travel and discussion that has grown around it from early on; it was live shows that built this band, and it traveled relentlessly to spread the music to new places. And so its fans have followed suit in an ever-growing caravan of thousands that follows where the music leads.

Ask fans how many DMB shows they've been to over the years, and you may hear numbers that creep well into the hundreds. Only in DMB-Land can someone who has seen twenty shows still be considered somewhat of a newbie. Time and time again, year after year (and some-times many times within a single year), DMB fans set off to places near and far to see their favorite band play as many shows as possible. One fan, Ahmad Zeki, explains this ravenous desire to see the band play everywhere and anywhere: "I've attended a hundred and six DMB shows since 1996. Every show has its own unique, diverse, eclectic sound. It's not merely a concert but rather an experience. After every show I'm left wanting more and more. There is something magical about this band."

With such massive show counts, it's clear that not all fans are going to see DMB play just in their own hometown venues. Call it Davecation, call it summer travel, but, like the Deadheads before them, DMB fans have a habit of hitting the road for their band. Of this lifestyle, one fan, Katie Ryan, says, "I haven't taken a 'normal' vacation for the past four years. All my trips are Davecations." Say what you will about the underlying purpose of these trips, but Davecations are inarguably a great way to see the world, and the DMB fan base in general tends to share a spirited affinity for travel and adventure. In 2009 alone, Ryan's voyages to see the band took her to Antwerp, Amsterdam, Manchester, and Dublin. Of her eclectic travel ven-tures she says, "I've been to places I never thought I'd go because of this band: Oklahoma, Nebraska, Texas, Belgium."

DMB often serves as the impetus fans need to book trips to places they've always wanted to see but haven't yet made it to. It's much more difficult to put off that vacation until some hazy point in the future when provided with a solid show date around which to build a trip. A fan since 1996, Mike Leone says that, for him, "Traveling with this band is a great way to multitask and an unbelievably good excuse to see parts of the world I wouldn't otherwise. I've been to some of the most legendary ven-ues in the States and saw two 2009 European shows, in Paris and Lucca. During the past sixteen years, DMB has been more than a band and music for me—it's led me to live my life in a way that I may not have otherwise.

I've traveled paths I may not otherwise have traveled, met people I may not have met, and it's afforded me the opportunity to create a mind full of experiences and stories. Stories that nobody else can tell, and experiences that nobody else can steal."

For college graduation from an art history program, Jared Smith had the opportunity to take his love for DMB and art on the road. Knowing that he'd always wanted to check out Italian Renaissance art first person, his brother presented him with two tickets to DMB's February 23, 2010, show in Rome for graduation. "What can I say except this was the new highlight of my life. I just graduated with an art history degree, and I'm going to what is pretty much Mecca for people like me, and, oh yeah, I'm *also* seeing my favorite band ever while I'm there! . . . I felt thrilled to share it with a bunch of fans, many of whom had probably never seen the band perform live before. Also, talk about getting to visit somewhere thanks to using DMB as an excuse!"

Bryan Narciso says, "DMB made me a more positive person. I began touring with DMB [in the 1990s], traveling, meeting so many close friends along the way—people I never would have met if it wasn't for this band. Just traveling, seeing this great country I live in, and meeting all these amazing people has made me want to live my life to the fullest."

In an effort to acquire such experiences, some fans hit the road very, very hard on an annual basis. Brad Adams says that over the past sixteen years he and his wife, Traci, "have amassed a lifetime of concert vacation memories, literally from all over the world." Of course, all of this comes at a price. Although DMB tickets are moderately priced in comparison to many of the major acts out there today, the cumulative total of tickets, travel, and lodging is no small expense—particularly when it's done multiple times per summer. But for DMB fans, where there's a will there's a way, and in many cases no distance is too far, no cost too high, to keep them out of the amphitheaters across the country where the music and magic are happening. Fans pull it off in any number of ways. Jeff Roberts explains his personal strategy for covering the costs of his DMB habit: "I even opened up a separate account called my Davings Account, which money automatically gets put into out of my weekly paycheck."

Perhaps most amazing when it comes to expenditures are the tapers. Every tour, tapers spend thousands of dollars traveling to venues across the country to record shows. Many of their recording rigs alone cost upward of $10,000—and this, of course, does not even begin to account for the significant additional expense of tickets and travel. Yet, for twenty years now, the high costs and lack of any financial compensation have not even remotely deterred tapers from this expensive hobby.

The motivations for taping vary from one person to the next and often change over time. John Kelly explains that, for him, it all stems from a love of concerts and the music itself. Personally, he says, "I want to make sure I can hear that concert I went to ten years from now." Bill Lakenan explains that, particularly in the pre-Internet days, "There was this real sense among tapers that you've got to at least do your part in getting this stuff out there. It was a prideful passion every time to spend ten or fifteen minutes breaking down your equipment while security was breathing over your shoulder."

Matt Yette has no doubt that both the band and the community would not be where they are today without the tapers who, while much appreciated among the ranks of DMB and the community, are somewhat unsung heroes outside this tight-knit circle. "It definitely takes a special kind of person to tape, and those guys take so much pride in what they do. I think we're fortunate to be in a community where management has let all of this go on indefinitely."

Another group that bears the brunt of a particularly high bill for showgoing are the foreign DMB fans who travel due to necessity. In order to achieve his twenty-six-show count, one Australian, David Moses, has made the trek from Down Under to the United States seven times to see DMB play live. Moses, who was introduced to DMB in 1997 by his little brother with the album *Crash,* says that being an Australian fan is "hard." "The band has only been here twice, in 2005 and 2007. I guess that's the motivation for traveling such huge distances to see the band play. They give us no choice! My wife and I have made some great friends in the U.S. through following DMB, and we're always looking forward to catching up with them."

Whether the travel is international or domestic, every year thousands of fans from remote locations make complex plans to travel to shows together. And for many, planning is half the fun. Though more recent DMB tours may span only a few months every summer, the community has developed its own calendar that takes up a vast portion of the year, what with obtaining tickets, coordinating travel groups, and setting up lodging plans. For many, the anticipation and communal planning process are almost as much of a bonding experience as the shows themselves. Dan Gardner says, "My second favorite day of the whole year, behind my wedding anniversary, is DMB Summer Tour Announcement Day." Scott Teuber, the proprietor of the Wildhorse Campground just outside the Gorge Amphitheatre in George, Washington, has witnessed the DMB calendar up close and personal due to the many fans who come flocking to his campground every year like clockwork for the band's three-night Labor Day weekend stand. "It's amazing—so many people make this Labor Day weekend the highlight of their summer and the highlight of their year. Occasionally I look at antsmarching.org, and in October, just a month after DMB left here, they're already planning their next trip. You look at the message boards in January, and they're counting down the days to the Gorge."

Chatting on message boards is often just a way to keep in touch during the touring off-season until the time when people gather face-to-face at the shows once again. One fan, Wendy Loo, who followed DMB around

North America hitting every single show of the 2002 spring, summer, and winter tours, essentially built an entire trip across a continent based on relationships begun on nancies.org that then transferred to "real life." Remembers Loo, "I coordinated with a lot of my friends online who lived in different parts of the country and were going to different shows. I lined up tickets and some places to stay. And then I just did it. I quit the law firm I was working at and just went for it." According to Loo, who documented her year on the road via the widely read website travelingnancy.org, walking away from her job and embarking on this adventure, which spanned 30,000 miles and seventy-seven shows, and required all of her savings, was worth it. "Honestly," she says, "the community played as big of a role in it as the music, if not more. I made a lot of lifetime friends, and funny things were always happening before and after the shows. Those things were just as important to me as the shows themselves. The music just brought people together. It was really about sharing experiences more than just being able to sing every word or meet Dave."

Though often on a smaller scale than Loo's, her story is a common one. Many DMB fans live by the rule that it's all about the journey, not the destination. One fan, Allison Cawley, fondly remembers making the nearly nine-hundred-mile trek from the July 1, 2010, Camden, New Jersey, show to DMB's next stop at the Alpine Valley Music Theatre in Wisconsin. "I left the morning after Camden with six of my friends for East Troy, Wisconsin. These seven people came from Pennsylvania, New Jersey, Washington, D.C., Utah, and New York. Some of us were good friends, some of us were familiar due to shows, and some of us had never met. But as always, we were brought together for one weekend of DMB. We drove sixteen hours, had a broccoli fight in traffic, shared drinks, set up tents, slathered suntan lotion on one another, sang until we had no voice, and experienced the beauty of Alpine Valley together. Why fly when you can have the best road trip ever?"

In the minds of fans, long road trips are a small price to pay for seeing a show. When the band is onstage, anything is fair game. You never know what show might hold an exciting debut, mark the reemergence of an oldie but goodie from the Liberation List, or contain a great moment of band-crowd interaction or a mind-bending jam. As opposed to many bands, which create a single set list for an entire tour, playing pretty much the same show every night, DMB mixes it up from one night to the next, leaving fans to wonder what will come next. One fan, Zachary Seiler, explains, "That's why we love them—because they put the live show first and give power over and above the studio. Because they do the things we love and hate. They tease us for months, they keep some things sacred and rare, and they rock the songs that they're supposed to night in and night out. It's why we'll travel miles to see the same band perform several times in the same summer. It's why when you see another fan on the street, you share that instant bond."

So great is the value of rare songs in the DMB realm that fan websites such as antsmarching.org and DMBAlmanac.com have created ranking systems, which rate a show's "rarity index" in the context of the entire tour. Fans can then compute their own personal rarity index and other stats based on the lifetime of shows they've attended. With this method, the higher your percentage rating is, the more obscure moments you've witnessed. In fact, with all of the online set list tracking and statistical calculations, DMB summer tours aren't that far off from America's other great summer pastime. This hunt is another part of what keeps longtime DMB fans in the game. Because of constant rotation, even veteran DMB fans still have wish lists of songs they have yet to hear. With all the shows he's seen in the past eighteen years, Nate Vandemark says, "At this point, all I'm doing is hunting down things I've never seen before."

In addition to statistics, DMB fans share another characteristic of baseball fans: tradition and ritual. Over the years, countless routines have arisen that are just as integral to the whole affair as the actual show itself.

Another fan, Jeremy Martin, explains his own DMB ritual, honed over the course of the fourteen years he's been following DMB: "Summer shows are by far my favorite, simply because of the tailgating. I am as ritualistic as the pope for shows. I must arrive no later than three P.M.—preferably two P.M., but some venues are pushing opening time further and further back. I have at least three courses of food that I cook, along with my blender for those wonderful boat drinks. The main ingredient, though, is the playlist (though it used to be mix CDs) of all the *other* bands and songs I love— there is a strict 'no Dave on Dave' rule for me. The playlist is always different and goes for almost the entire tailgating session. Then, with thirty-five minutes before the walk to the show, the game-time mix is played. This playlist is more predictable and always closes with James Brown's 'Sex Machine.' These songs are always the ones that any human with a pulse cannot help but move to. I have been asked many times to play DMB during tailgating, and though I don't knock those who do, I cannot. The best way to describe my philosophy is: When I go out for a great meal, I don't order the same thing for an appetizer as I do for an entree."

It goes without saying that the live shows and the traveling they often entail go back to the whole community aspect of the DMB fan base. The summer months offer a rare opportunity for the many friendships that have built up around this band to be transferred to "real life." While communication occurs online all year long, it's at the shows that people really have the chance to come together and celebrate, even if it's only for one night. As one fan, Erika Price, puts it, "DMB is more than just music; it is family, friends, memories, and something to look forward to all winter long. I count down the days until the boys of summer will bring us all together again."

Because of this sense of communal gathering, the parking lots and preshow meet-ups are just as much of a draw as the shows themselves. It's in this time, before the stage lights go up, that old friends have the chance to come together and hang out and new friendships are fostered.

Jeff Roberts explains, "I have continued traveling the country to follow DMB and will continue until there is no more. The DMB community is a family, and I have met so many of my friends while tailgating three to four hours before a show. It's an amazing experience and amazing time with an *unbelievably* large family. People say I'm obsessed with DMB, but I just tell them: it's not an obsession; it's a way of life." Kaysie Bowman concurs. "It sounds funny, but I almost enjoy the fans as much as I enjoy the band. The preconcert is just as fun as the concert. The fan base makes you feel like you're part of something, connected in a way, through this great music, to thousands of other people that you would never know if it wasn't for this band. Every DMB concert experience I have had so far has been a great one. There is just such a positive energy in the venue, and almost everybody in the audience is getting along and just having a great time. Everybody is able to put differences aside and just have an awesome night."

Gatherings extend outside the parking lots as well. As an offshoot of connections made on the nancies.org message board, Jeff Watts of Charlotte, North Carolina, offered to host a preconcert gathering at his home for a group of far-flung fans in 2000. More than a decade later, this gathering has become an annual tradition. Says Watts, "We have had people attend from several different foreign countries and from all over the U.S. We've met lifelong friends who we maintain contact with throughout the year and meet up with for concerts in other cities."

There is a strange sort of juxtaposition that comes with this travel. Although the point of travel is to see new scenery and escape life's day-to-day routine, the community gatherings and familiar sights and sounds of shows create a certain sort of "coming home" for fans, despite the fact that they are actually often quite far from home. Joey LaCroix explains, "When I go to a DMB show, I feel more than at home. I know that everyone around me understands the way I feel when I hear the strumming of 'Dreaming Tree' or the snap of Carter's snare drum on 'Ants.' At every show, I get the same feeling I got the first time I saw them; it's that feeling that, for the next three hours, nothing can go wrong. It's just you, the band, and twenty thousand of your closest friends." Brenda Gonzalez very much agrees that DMB shows feel like a second home. She explains, "You know when you've been on a trip and you're dying to go home? Even if you're having a really good time, you just start to think, I really want to be in my house, around familiar things. When I go to a show, it's like that. It's familiar but not in a boring way. It's like coming home. It's, like, this is what I know, this is where I'm comfortable, this is where I forget everything. No matter what's going on, this is where I want to be. With these people I don't even know, who I feel a sense of community with, the person you end up sitting next to, you might end up staying at their house next year. It's really weird because you miss it—when DMB isn't touring, you miss it. But you're not just missing the shows, you're missing everything. You miss seeing your friends, you miss the traveling, you miss the whole scene."

There is an extremely intangible yet compelling element to the experience. DMB shows have the strange ability to create an odd sort of bubble around the tiny, temporary world that only band and community inhabit, albeit for a short amount of time. And inside this bubble, there's nothing but music, celebration, and friendship. For the space of a few hours, everything else is left outside. One fan, Nick Falcone, says, "Over the years my family and friends have asked me, 'Why do you go to see the same band multiple times a year? Isn't it the same show?' My response is always the same: I tell them a DMB show is the only place in the world where I can forget all my troubles and worries for the next three hours, beginning the moment I walk through those venue gates. This band and their music have provided me with some of the best times and memories in my life over the past ten years and have also helped me through some of the roughest times in my life. I have met some extraordinarily wonderful people at these shows and consider them my DMB family."

Stefan Lessard offers his take on the lure the shows and road have on fans each and every summer: "For me, it's kind of like camp. Every summer I come out, and it's the same people. You have your catering and cooking, you have your activities you're supposed to be doing and your times you're supposed to be there and this and that. It's like very structured camp. And then, at the same time, for fans it's kinda like camp but it's like Memorial Day. It's days you get to go with your friends and family and do something fun."

And of course, after all of this traveling and hanging out and celebrating, there's still the actual show. Chris LoMauro explains the experience from his perspective: "Every time I see DMB, I enjoy the first ten minutes of the show the most. That moment when the lights go out and the crowd gets louder and louder . . . the hairs on my neck stand up, and an unrestrainable smile grows across my face. And then the band walks out. The crowd gets so loud that you can feel the ground shaking. In that moment and for the rest of the show, you feel like a part of something. Part of a crowd of thousands, coming to salute the guys that help us get through hard times and to enjoy the good times even more. It's the greatest show on earth, and everyone knows it."

Over the course of the past twenty years, there have been countless moments at shows all around the world that have left fans alternately roaring and speechless. Many would argue that there is a euphoric, unforgettable moment at pretty much every show DMB plays, whether in Wichita, Kansas, or New York City. But over time, some venues have become legendary must-see stops for every DMB fan to check off his or her to-do list. Which is precisely why you find such a high percentage of DMB fans who can tell you all about places like East Troy, Wisconsin; George, Washington; and Saratoga Springs, New York. Though none of these towns may be tourist destinations for the average citizen, they happen to house Alpine, the Gorge, and SPAC, respectively—affectionately dubbed the Big Three venues.

If the DMB world had a Mecca, there's a good argument that the Gorge Amphitheatre would be it. For those who follow the band around, chances are it's just a matter of time until they make their way to this venue. Located in the desolate reaches of eastern Washington about three hours away from Seattle, the Gorge is truly one of a kind. DMB began playing the Gorge in 1996 (its first appearance there was as part of the H.O.R.D.E. line-up) and has returned every year since; mostly, in recent years, the Gorge stop has consisted of a three-night stand over Labor Day weekend. For many fans, the Gorge is the culmination of the summer tour and the chance to meet up with friends from far-flung locations across the United States.

Nature is such an integral part of the Gorge experience that the venue has almost a sacred, spiritual feeling. Upon entering the seating area of the amphitheater, fans are greeted with a sprawling view of the Columbia River below. David Spiegelman remembers the experience of walking into the Gorge for the first time: "I was taken aback by the sheer magnitude of my favorite band and our following out here on the cliff of the Columbia Gorge, in the middle of nowhere, about to rock for three days." The stage seems to be almost part of the landscape, set among the cliffs and overlooks that make up the Gorge. As the show starts, with the music floating out into the night air while the sun sets behind the stage, it's clear why Dave Matthews himself has referred to the venue as "Heaven's Amphitheater." Ahmad Zeki explains, "These shows are the most magical, with the beautiful scenery of the Columbia River, the gorge, the experience of camping and river rafting. It makes the whole experience one big outdoor event, never to be missed."

Because of its remote and scenic location, Gorge concertgoers tend to immerse themselves in the atmosphere for three days during Labor Day weekend. With campgrounds located on-site and just outside the perimeter of the amphitheater and the Columbia River offering plenty of activities to fill an entire day, most fans tend to remain close to home base, moving from the campgrounds to the river to the venue and then back again for three days in a row.

For the past few years, one fan, Brian Toups, has been bringing a group of dozens who originally met online together for the annual Gorge shows. So entrenched is this tradition of planning and camping together that this group of Gorge regulars has dubbed itself "Toupstown." Says Toups, "I really enjoy bringing people together, and now I have these friends that are all over the world. The only time I get to see them is when we go to a show. I've met roommates that way. My girlfriend and I met at the Gorge. It started out as this online message board and became a close-knit circle of real-life friends that have become part of my life forever."

Across the country in Saratoga Springs, New York, the setting is much different. If you didn't know what you were looking for, you might be a bit surprised to find the Saratoga Performing Arts Center (SPAC) nestled in the middle of a state park in the midst of this quaint town. The amphitheater itself is unconventional, with covered pavilion seating that extends sharply upward and is higher than the lawn area.

In addition to the venue's unique setup, DMB's annual two-night stands there have a reputation for stellar set lists and a rowdy crowd. Brad Casacci, who has hit every SPAC show since 2001, says, "After being [at] nineteen venues all across the country and forty-eight shows, SPAC is still my favorite venue because of how vocal and knowledgeable the fans are in regards to DMB and because of the chemistry and interaction between the band and fans. DMB typically plays some of their better shows (for the hard-core fans) at SPAC to show their appreciation for the fan base that comes out to the venue." It's not only fans that love the venue—the band does too. As Dave said on July 2, 2005, "It's always good to come here. I tell ya, Roi and I were talking about it—this room and this crowd got a great energy every year we come here, so thank you very much."

Nearly a thousand miles westward, set amid a vast expanse of farmland in East Troy, Wisconsin, Alpine Valley Music Theatre is one of those places that just seems to breed high energy, from its parking lots to the actual venue. Though there's obviously a feeling of excitement before *every* show at *every* venue, at Alpine the excitement is an entity in and of itself. More than 35,000 fans pour into the color-coded parking lots many hours before the show, their beanbag-toss games in tow. Stefan Lessard observes, "I'm on the stage side, I'm not out there really experiencing the community hangout, but when I was in Alpine I did a video segment for MySpace and I was up near the top of Alpine. From there I saw fans setting up all their games and everything that happens in the lots at Alpine. It was just really cool."

For several hours it's playtime . . . and then it's showtime. Showtime at Alpine is a force unto itself, with the band and audience engaged in a constant back-and-forth, which ultimately spins the venue energy to a mind-bending fever pitch. One of the greatest examples of this back-and-forth occurred over the course of two years, at DMB's 2008 and 2009 Alpine stops. Sean Orti, there both years, remembers watching it all go down. "On night two in 2008, as DMB closed with 'Thank You,' the crowd participation was so great I still get chills thinking about it. We must have continued singing 'Thank You' for what seems a half hour after DMB walked offstage. The lights came on, the crew broke down the set, the ushers were asking people to leave, and we were all still singing. Then came night two at Alpine in 2009. With the end of last year still fresh in our minds, before DMB came back onstage for the encore, the crowd started singing 'Thank You' again. And again it was so loud that it gives me chills for a second time. As DMB walked onstage, you could see that they were enjoying it, egging the crowd along. And then they joined in with the crowd, kicking into a crazy impromptu version of 'Thank You.' There are far too few moments of pure joy in life. Moments that are perfect and you can just feel the happiness fill up inside of you. That's what this was like for me. With the thirty-odd-thousand people all singing the same thing and loving life, it really was a moment that I will cherish forever. That's what DMB can do for you, and that's why I can't imagine my life without this band."

With the intensity of these shared experiences both in the parking lots and online, marriages, babies, and friendships that are built to stand the test of time have found their roots in the DMB community. Ron and Ally Whitworth met online in the official DMB fan club Warehouse chat room on the day it opened. Several years later, the two married. Says Ron, "Despite living in different cities, we ended up meeting one weekend and were married a year and a half later. Without DMB, we never would have met." Likewise, Jose Mendoza says, "My wife and I are tied to DMB. It's one of the foundations of our marriage, as crazy as that sounds. We've been going to shows for the past ten years and celebrated our eleventh wedding anniversary at the July 31, 2010, show at West Palm Beach. We lived the music in college, and, as we have grown, the music has had more of an impact on our lives."

Of course, the fan base also feels a great connection with the band itself, a sentiment with which Stefan can relate. "If you think about it, I was about sixteen when this band started. And a lot of these other hard-core fans were probably, if not my age, a little older. They were probably in college. I feel like I've been *raised* by this band. And I think . . . that our music has affected people at different moments of their life over the past twenty years. And the same goes for me and for everyone else in the band. Everything in my life from the time I was sixteen to now can be somewhat related to what was happening with the band. In that sense, it's like I've kind of been raised by a pack of wolves and this is sort of who I am and who I've turned out to be. And the ones that I can relate to the most are the fans who have been there too—who understand that."

To its great credit, DMB has created an atmosphere that really fosters a sense of connection with its audience, even in the most massive of venues. As Matt McKibben puts it, "There's a definite give-and-take, and the band and community both feed off one another." Spontaneous in nature, DMB is the type of act that can turn on a dime. Countless times, audiences have risen up with a chanted plea for a song and the band has veered completely off course of the set list, right there in the moment along with the crowd.

So well established is this back-and-forth between band and crowd that over the years crowd-based traditions have formed and are repeated annually at pretty much every venue across the country. For example, the audience knows precisely when it's their turn to start chanting "Woo!" at the beginning of "Warehouse." Everyone knows that if "Everyday" is played, the audience provides the background interpolation of "#36." Fans who hear "The Stone" played live pitch in with Elvis Presley's "Only Fools Rush In" chorus during the outro. Every now and then the crowd picks up the lead vocals altogether for "Jimi Thing." And, of course, what show would be complete without a nice, rowdy chant for "Halloween" during the encore? Many a newbie has looked around in complete and utter confusion at the thousands of fans on their feet, stomping and yelling for "Halloween" at the top of their lungs in the middle of July. And should you actually witness a "Halloween," be ready for all hell to break loose. Allison Cawley remembers that when she heard "Halloween" live for the first time at SPAC on June 13, 2009, "I had a broken leg at the show, and when I heard the opening notes of 'Halloween' I threw down my crutches and started running in circles."

Whether you're a new fan or a veteran, young or old, American or any other nationality, there's always room for more in the DMB community. McKibben observes, "It's a weird cocktail of people—you would think a potentially *violent* cocktail, but not so much. You have the frat boys on one end of the spectrum, and then, on the complete other end of the spectrum, you have your hippies. That was one of the most intriguing things to me when I first discovered the band—that two of the least likely groups of people to be hanging out were, in fact, hanging out. The music brings totally opposite groups of people together and speaks to their inherent similarities; the music brings us back together."

Jeff Cunningham, who went to several Grateful Dead shows before finding DMB, says that this diversity is part of the appeal for him. "What attracted me so much to the DMB fan base was the gamut of people. It's not all tie-dye-wearing people. It's doctors, and lawyers, and druggies. White collar and blue collar. It's just the whole spectrum. And the Dead fans were pretty much all the same. I used to go to Dead shows and didn't want to be a poser and wear tie-dye for the occasion, so I would wear my polo shirts and beat around the parking lot and everyone thought I was a cop."

A wide age range can also be found at DMB shows—in fact, more so every year as die-hard fans become parents themselves. Fans who began seeing the band in college have now moved into adulthood and started families. With this, for some DMB shows have evolved into somewhat of a family tradition. In 1994, McKibben's father gave him his first DMB CD, *Under the Table and Dreaming*. McKibben's son, in turn, was raised on DMB. In 2010, at just fourteen years old, McKibben's son already has eight shows under his belt. Initially, McKibben was somewhat apprehensive about taking his son to a concert, despite their mutual love of the band. "I wanted to take him to a show, but I was worried about it. We listen to the music all the time, and he wanted to go. Finally I broke down when he was eight, but I was stressed out about it. I picked a quiet place on the lawn for us, looked around, and realized that in our area of the lawn there was nothing but little kids. Now I notice it more and more every year; the people who bring their kids to the show kind of gather together, and out there on the lawn at a rock 'n' roll show, the community forms a kid-safe zone. I think that's a real testament to the community."

Christopher Smith has also made DMB shows a family affair. He remembers, "In 1997, two months after my son was born, I traveled more than fifteen hundred miles with my brother to Morrison, Colorado, to see DMB play Red Rocks. I stood there under the clear sky and listened with tears in my eyes to 'Lie in Our Graves.' I was scared out of my mind at the responsibility of fatherhood, and listening to this band play the song I used as a lullaby for my son brought a sense of calm to me. In 2001 I took my son to Texas Stadium to see his first show. I held him on my shoulder and sang along while the band played 'his' song. He may not be able to remember it, but I will for the rest of my life."

Over time the DMB community has banded together on many occasions for many causes. But every now and then—and especially when the going gets rough—it unites in big and heartwarming ways. In June 2009 the community suffered a loss when a longtime fan, Matt Wadleigh, passed away at age thirty. Particularly in southern California DMB circles, Wadleigh was a familiar face based on a homemade sign he debuted at the August 26, 2004, Chula Vista, California, show and brought with him to every show he attended thereafter. The sign read simply: LoVE.

A fan since 1994, Wadleigh traveled from coast-to-coast (and to many states in between) to see his favorite band play. Wadleigh's best friend from high school, Darren Raymond, fondly remembers one of those early DMB ventures: "I particularly remember a show at Giants Stadium when a terrible thunderstorm rolled through. Matt just stood there focused on the band, smiling the whole time while getting unbelievably soaked. Most of the crowd went running for cover and missed some of the most amazing music of the night." According to his longtime friend and fellow DMB fan Dawn Mitschele, "DMB was a huge part of Matt's life, and his love and commitment for the band only grew over the years." Mitschele believes that Wadleigh's deep loyalty to the band stemmed from the fact that "DMB collectively expressed all the joy, all the love, and all the celebration that Matt felt for life."

It was with that in mind that Wadleigh made his first LoVE sign in the Chula Vista parking lot before the show in 2004. Mitschele remembers, "He shared that he had this vision of himself holding a sign that simply said 'LoVE' on it. Matt felt it was the one word that encapsulated the soul of Dave's music, and Matt wanted to reflect his love back to Dave and the band onstage. We drew the sign out right then and there in the parking lot. I remember the first time he ever held it up. It was when Dave first walked out onto the stage for his set, and he pointed right at Matt and his sign. That was it for Matt. He continued to bring that sign to every show after that night, making new ones when the old ones got too worn out to hold." Up until his last show at the MGM Grand Garden Arena in Las Vegas on May 9, 2009, Wadleigh continued to proudly display his message of LoVE. "One of my favorite memories is of the last show I ever saw with Matt," says Mitschele. "I distinctly remember watching him as he held up his LoVE sign and thinking to myself, He's holding it with as much excitement, intention, generosity, and joy as if it were the very first time. I also remember looking over at him as he was dancing—he was glowing and grinning from ear to ear, radiant and filled with complete joy. I actually stopped to watch him and take it in. It is one of the most beautiful memories I have of seeing my friend enjoying his favorite band on Earth."

In the days following Wadleigh's death, duplicate LoVE signs began cropping up at DMB shows across the country, to the point where there were often a number of LOVE signs present at any given show. Matthews himself paid tribute to Wadleigh, introducing "Lie in Our Graves" at the June 17, 2009, Maryland Heights, Missouri, show by saying "This song is for my late friend Matt. He used to come to the show and hold up a sign that said LoVE. And it was good. Every time I saw that sign I'd think, Man, that's a generous gift just to come and show a sign that says nothing but LoVE. And I just want to send this song out to him and all of his in gratitude for that generosity. And rest in peace, my brother."

In August 2009 Kayla Fisher-Poling organized what has since become known as the traveling LoVE sign. Fisher-Poling made an easily transportable duplicate of Wadleigh's LoVE sign on a pillowcase and set up a system whereby fans could sign up to hold the sign at one show and pass it off to another fan, who would then take it on to the next show. In this way, the sign was passed from one fan to the next, making its way through the remainder of the 2009 North American tour. "Someone told me the sign is like the Olympic torch of DMB," Fisher-Poling says with a laugh. Each person who held the LoVE sign signed his or her name on the back, as did almost all of the band members who caught on to the community's tribute to Wadleigh. A new version of the LoVE sign continued in 2010, hopping across the pond for DMB's spring 2010 European tour and continuing on to crisscross the United States and Canada for DMB's 2010 North American tour.

The goodwill extends outside the DMB community in more global ways as well. Over the years the band has instituted an increasing number of eco-friendly measures to ensure that both their touring practices and their shows are as environmentally low impact as possible. Through its Bama Green Project, DMB has teamed up with Reverb (a nonprofit program that promotes green touring) and Stefan's IZStyle to both educate and promote green measures among its fan base and to take steps toward making its tours as eco-friendly as possible. The band has instituted a number of programs in an effort to do this, including a carbon offset program (which has kept 7,200,000 pounds of carbon monoxide from being generated); utilization of biodiesel on buses and rigs (75,000 gallons to date); recycling programs; and car-pool programs for fans attending shows (which has kept 2,352,000 pounds of carbon monoxide from being generated). Additionally, fans are invited to volunteer at Eco Villages, set up at each show to teach other fans about greening measures that can be taken both at the concerts and in their own lives.

In addition to the Bama Green efforts, Stefan has been able to leverage his relationship with fans to bring the community together for good causes that are important to him. In September 2009, for example, he teamed up with Surfrider Foundation and a team of DMB fans to clean up San Diego's Ocean Beach. Of his interest in this, Lessard says, "I grew up in Charlottesville, so I was always involved with the Rivana River Society, which hosts river cleanups. Growing up, I had a really cool science teacher, and we'd go do stream cleanups and check out the ecology of the stream and pick up trash and stuff like that. I started surfing when I moved out to California and was seeing plastic and bottles in the water; then I'd go on the beach and see cigarette butts and trash and plastic—I don't like this. So I joined Surfrider and started finding out about all the beach cleanups they do. The fan cleanup in San Diego was perfect—it was just awesome and something that I'd love to do more of. I think we had about a hundred participants in San Diego, and it was *amazing* how much trash we picked up. I actually somewhat enjoy it. I used to love rummaging around the dump when I was a kid. I'd always be rummaging around the stream and picking up weird stuff. So for me it's kind of fun."

In the end, that's what it all comes down to: the DMB community is a community with a conscience and a heart. Onstage, the band's music and lyrics joyfully celebrate love, kindness, and brotherhood. The spirit of this message has trickled down through the community, and when the community is at its very best, it reflects that message right back out at the band and the rest of the world.

Though there are any number of bands with loyal followings, there is something unique about the DMB fan base. Wildhorse Campground proprietor Scott Teuber, who sees thousands of music fans of all stripes come through the Gorge every year, says that the collective personality of the DMB community is evident even from an outsider's perspective. "The first year that I was open, when it came time for DMB I was totally shocked by how far people traveled—we had people come from Japan and Germany and just about every state in the U.S. Thirteen years later, it still amazes me—the culture and just the way people are. The biggest difference I see between DMB fans and other fans is that truly they're all friends that have just not yet met. It's truly the definition of 'there are no strangers here.'"

CHAPTER 10

LOOKING BACK

I FIND IT HARD TO EXPLAIN HOW I GOT HERE

Twenty years after DMB began, many things have changed. Demolished in 2002, Trax no longer exists. Other bands that came onto the music scene at the same time as DMB are long defunct. And, of course, even DMB itself looks much different than it once did with the absence of LeRoi Moore and incorporation of touring members Rashawn Ross and Jeff Coffin.

According to the Charlottesville journalist David McNair, even the town that gave birth to DMB is no longer as it once was. "Coran Capshaw is a huge person in the music business now and owns a ton of real estate. There's so many big players in the music business here now. There's a lot of other music venues now too. On the Downtown Mall there's the pavilion that Capshaw built and also a theater [Jefferson Theater] that he just renovated that's also a music venue. So there're two big music venues downtown that Capshaw built and DMB is ultimately responsible for."

Not only has new architecture risen throughout Charlottesville since DMB was coming up, but McNair believes that its musical reputation has as well. "We have an embarrassment of riches now in terms of big music acts that come in here. I think it's connected with DMB. You know, the Rolling Stones played here. U2 played here. We're just this little town—there are only forty thousand people here. But people in the music business have their base here, and they're able to convince these big acts to come through." Of Charlottesville's increased visibility on the music landscape, a September 2006 article in *The Hook* noted, ". . . we have these five to thank for all this. Charlottesville birthed DMB, and DMB birthed Charlottesville as the cultural epicenter that it has become. Great art can grow anywhere. Might as well be here."

Over the years, DMB has done much more than just growing the Charlottesville music scene. Since the inception of its Bama Works Fund in 1999, the band has donated more than $8.5 million to local charities, causes, and music programs. Additionally, the LeRoi Moore Fund (founded after his death) continues to contribute money to many of the causes and organizations he supported during his life as well as provide scholarships to select local recipients.

For those who knew DMB when it was a fledgling band, there's a temptation to analyze history, to search for clues that this offbeat bar band would make it as big as it did and last for as long as it has. But, according to Col. Bruce Hampton, no matter how musically proficient or charming it was, the path DMB ultimately took was unpredictable at the offset. Says Hampton, "I never thought it would last this long or be this big."

In fact, even Dave Matthews was wary of the road ahead. As he told the Baton Rouge *Advocate* on February 17, 1995, "For health of mind, I'm imagining that our descent could come any time. It is flattering to have people enjoying what we do, but it certainly won't last forever. I have to keep a perspective on it because it will pass, and the glamour of it will pass. I hope I can find the lessons that come out of it."

For others, though, the fact that something was about to happen was more obvious, even in the earliest days. When asked if he thought DMB would go big, Mark Lynn, who started seeing DMB in 1991, responds, "Absolutely. The thing that's so strange is I really do not generally like the type of music DMB plays, although I liked them then and now. But it's just so bizarre that I would get into it the first place. It was so obviously not calculated and such an organic thing. You go to your first show, and there's this really strange guy with a weird voice saying dumb shit between the songs. Then they've got a violin player and a powerhouse of a drummer and this young, skinny kid playing bass. How the hell does this happen? Strangely enough, it's something that worked. It really worked because of them and because they worked their asses off."

No matter how big DMB has become, though, certain things have remained constant over the years. Throughout two decades, DMB retained much of its original road crew, bringing them from the bars and coffee shops of Virginia all the way to Central Park's Great Lawn. As musicians, they have preserved a certain spryness that many bands lose over time; even twenty years later, things still remain fresh and unpredictable onstage. And the grassroots marketing that helped propel DMB to the top is still very much in place through the ongoing practice of taping and trading, in whatever form they may take as technology speeds along. But most of all, the fans are still there—certainly there are many more than there were in the early days, but they maintain the same devotion and excitement that helped spread the word from Charlottesville all the way to Australia.

Most impressive, the band members themselves have not changed much. Quite simply, as one local journalist wrote in a June 2007 issue of *C-Ville*, "In all my years here, I don't think I've ever, not once, heard a single person say that the DMB guys were anything but the nicest guys in the world." Though they now rank among the most successful musicians in the world, their demeanor continues to defy rock star stereotypes. There is a palpable sense of awe among the band members every night as they take the stage and look out at the massive audience spread before them. In turn, fans continue to be floored by the music, time and time again, show after show after show.

For twenty years straight, DMB has remained relevant and progressive in an industry that is fickle and ever changing. This has been accomplished through a unique combination of classic old-school tactics and the foresight to remain flexible and adapt to the changing technology and advancements that have taken DMB all the way from Memorex to MP3. And, of course, timing is everything. Technology has certainly played a role in all of this as well. Antsmarching.org cofounder Matt Yette muses, "Basically, you're talking the modern-day Grateful Dead in terms of grassroots support, and the Internet just started taking off at the right time for them. The Internet has become such a large part of it all. Could this band be as big as it is without technology? No, not in this day and age."

When David McNair looks back, he finds it hard to believe that twenty years have passed and things have progressed so far beyond those Tuesday-night Trax shows. Watching a once-obscure local act rise to such levels of success, he says, has been nothing short of unbelievable. "This [type of success] is a once-in-a-lifetime—or once-in-a-*three*-lifetime— event. It's *very, very* rare. It's mind-blowing. This does not happen—the odds of it are just so minuscule."

For Matt McKibben, the past twenty years can't be explained purely by the tangibles such as the power of the music, the dedication of the fan base, or the progression of technology, though all of these elements have certainly played a role in the success DMB has enjoyed. "I would say it has very little to do with the music, actually, though that's obviously the catalyst. Throughout all of this, I think the guys themselves—they've got the right makeup, they were born to do what they're doing right now. And it's really exciting to be a part of something like this because it doesn't happen all that often. I think it's impossible for them *not* to play. So often I remind people, be grateful—DMB doesn't have to play. They're doing it because they're supposed to be doing it. It's chemistry. It's having the right makeup, and they've just got it."

But no matter how unlikely the whole twenty-year story of DMB has been thus far, it *did* happen—and twenty years later, DMB and its fans are still here dancing.

DISCOGRAPHY (1993–2010)

STUDIO RELEASES

Remember Two Things (Bama Rags, November 1993; rerelease RCA, June 1997)

Recently EP (Bama Rags, 1994; rerelease RCA, 1997)

Under the Table and Dreaming (September 1994)

Crash (April 1996)

Before These Crowded Streets (April 1998)

Everyday (February 2001)

Busted Stuff (July 2002)

Stand Up (May 2005)

The Best of What's Around, Vol. 1 (November 2006)

Big Whiskey and the GrooGrux King (June 2009)

LIVE WIDE RELEASE

Live at Red Rocks 8.15.95 (October 1997)

Live at Luther College [Dave Matthews and Tim Reynolds] (January 1999)

*Listener Supported** (November 1999)

Live in Chicago 12.19.98 (October 2001)

*Live at Folsom Field, Boulder, Colorado** (November 2002)

*The Central Park Concert** (November 2003)

*The Gorge** (June 2004)

*Weekend on the Rocks** (November 2005)

*Live at Radio City** (August 2007)

*Live at Piedmont Park** (December 2007)

Live at Mile High Music Festival (December 2008)

*Europe 2009** (December 2009)

Live in Las Vegas [Dave Matthews and Tim Reynolds] (February 2010)

Live in New York City (November 2010)

*CD and DVD release

LIVE TRAX SERIES

Vol. 1, Centrum Center, Worcester, Massachusetts, 12.8.98 (November 2004)

Vol. 2, Golden Gate Park, San Francisco, California, 9.12.04 (December 2004)

Vol. 3, Meadows Music Theatre, Hartford, Connecticut, 8.27.00 (March 2005)

Vol. 4, Classic Amphitheatre, Richmond, Virginia, 4.30.96 (September 2005)

Vol. 5, Meadow Brook Music Festival, Rochester Hills, Michigan, 8.23.95 (May 2006)

Vol. 6, Fenway Park, Boston, Massachusetts, 7.7.06 and 7.8.06 (September 2006)

Vol. 7, Hampton Coliseum, Hampton, Virginia, 12.31.96 (December 2006)

Vol. 8, Alpine Valley Music Theatre, East Troy, Wisconsin, 8.7.04 (March 2007)

Vol. 9, MGM Grand Garden Arena, Las Vegas, Nevada, 3.23.07 and 3.24.07 (June 2007)

Vol. 10, Pavilhão Atlântico, Lisbon, Portugal, 5.25.07 (November 2007)

Vol. 11, Saratoga Performing Arts Center, Saratoga Springs, New York, 8.29.00 (March 2008)

Vol. 12, L. B. Day Amphitheatre, Salem, Oregon, 5.5.95 (July 2008)

Vol. 13, Busch Stadium, St. Louis, Missouri, 6.7.08 (December 2008)

Vol. 14, Nissan Pavilion at Stone Ridge, Bristow, Virginia, 6.28.08 (March 2009)

Vol. 15, Alpine Valley Music Theatre, East Troy, Wisconsin, 8.9.08 (June 2009)

Vol. 16, Riverbend Music Center, Cincinnati, Ohio, 6.26.00 (September 2000)

Vol. 17, Shoreline Amphitheatre, Mountain View, California, 7.06.97 (May 2009)

Vol. 18, GTE Virginia Beach Amphitheater, Virginia Beach, Virginia, 6.4.96 (August 2010)

Vol. 19, Vivo Rio, Rio de Janeiro, Brazil, 9.30.08 (November 2010)

Live Trax (compilation, Vols. 1–9; exclusive to Starbucks) (July 2007)

Live Trax 2008 [free digital download for Summer 2008 concert attendees who purchased tickets via Ticketmaster or Warehouse] (November 2008)

DMB LIVE SERIES
(AVAILABLE FROM DMBand.COM ONLY)

Prism Coffeehouse, Charlottesville, Virginia, 4.22.93 [Dave Matthews and Tim Reynolds] (December 2008)

Town Point Park, Norfolk, Virginia, 4.26.94 (December 2008)

Blue Note, Colombia, Missouri, 10.22.94 (December 2008)

China Club, New York, New York, 1.9.04 [Dave Matthews] (December 2008)

Benaroya Hall, Seattle, Washington, 10.24.02 [Dave Matthews] (December 2008)

Irving Plaza, New York, New York, 3.26.94 (July 2009)

Appalachian State University, Boone, North Carolina, 3.29.03 [Dave Matthews and Tim Reynolds] (September 2009)

The Bayou, Washington, D.C., 4.10.93 (September 2009)

Warfield Theatre, San Francisco, California, 5.10.95 (September 2009)

The Flood Zone, Richmond, Virginia, 1.27.93 (November 2009)

Frank Erwin Center, Austin, Texas, 10.24.96 (February 2010)

The Bayou, Washington, D.C., 12.21.92 (June 2010)

Kirby Fieldhouse (Lafayette College), Easton, Pennsylvania, 2.25.95 (September 2010)

SOLO RELEASES

True Reflections [Boyd Tinsley] (RCA, June 2003)

Some Devil [Dave Matthews] (RCA, September 2003)

ACKNOWLEDGMENTS

It sounds trite, but it's all too true in the case of this book that there are way too many helpful hands in the DMB community to cite—I've been blown away. A big, wholly inadequate shout-out to y'all. Special recognition to my great pal Rob Banagale and Jake Vigliotti, both of who have been beyond helpful throughout the writing process. Also, to all those behind-the-scenes characters who have spent innumerable hours working on (among others) antsmarching.org, nancies.org, DMBAlmanac.com, and DreamingTree.org, so that we can all have this band's vibrant history right at our fingertips.

Thanks to my agent, Coleen O'Shea, for all her help putting this project together, seeing it through from start to finish, and, most of all, for finding it the perfect home. Thanks to my editor, Michelle Howry, for her patience, calm voice, and discerning eye. Also to the fabulous Simon & Schuster team, including Alex Preziosi, Jessica Chin, and Ruth Lee-Mui.

To my amazing friend and locker partner of yore, Andrea Diaz-Vaughn, a truckload of thanks for the many skills you've offered up throughout the course of this project, including: Web design, neuroses-checking, and, most of all, keeping it real. I'm sure you are shuddering at the general inconciseness that fills these pages.

To my favorite ladies, Maria Gagliano and Celia Johnson, for lending their expert eyes and warm hearts to this and every other professional and personal endeavor in my life over the course of the past six years. It was a lucky day for me when our book-wormy paths crossed.

Thanks to Ty, for being a sounding board dating back to when this project was just a seedling.

To my aunt Binky (a.k.a. Kathleen Seabolt) who probably had no idea she was setting the tone for my entire life with all of the books she siphoned my way throughout my childhood. I will always be grateful.

To my host of girlfriends aside from those already mentioned, who have created the world's best support system and extended family over the years and who have doggedly continued to love me, even in my most un-lovable moments: Allison Starks, Angela Koech, Anne Chatfield, Cal Horton, Denise "Sternad" Reid, Jen Durkin, Laura Brown, Meg "Coach" Schuck, and Natalie Bubalo—I'm talking to you, kids. Also to Rick Patri and Matt Cochrane who, though not girls, have nonetheless been a couple of my best buddies and partners in crime for fifteen years and counting.

Most of all and above all else, to Mom and Dad, who gave me the greatest gift by teaching me that all things are possible and for never, for a single second, letting me doubt how loved I am. Thank you for being the best parents, friends, shoulders to cry on, proofreaders, and DMB fans a girl could ask for.